I'm Supposed to Make a Difference

A Memoir About Overcoming Trauma and Abuse

Kevin Vought

I'm Supposed to Make a Difference

A Memoir About Overcoming Trauma and Abuse

ISBN: 978-1-7365238-7-2

Cover Design by: Michael Rehder / rehderandcompanie.com

Edited by: Jocelyn Carbonara

Acknowledgments

I'd first and foremost like to thank my wife, Jill Vought, for her decades of devotion, patience, guidance, and loving support. Without her, I can without a doubt say I wouldn't be who I am right now. She stood by me through many dark and ugly days, weeks, and months while I sorted out troubling memories that were roaring back to me. I even redirected a lot of that ugliness at her, unleashing hate and venom toward her that nobody should ever have to absorb. She always shrugged off the verbal attacks, knowing it wasn't me driving them, but the demons of my past I was so diligently battling. I don't even begin to deserve to have her in my life, yet here she still is.

I'd also like to thank my psychologist, Dr. Mary Watson, PhD, who spent over ten years helping me make sense of memory fragments from long ago as they came back into clearer focus. She provided one of the first reviews of this book and was so impressed, she offered to write a very meaningful foreword. I never would have had the strength or knowledge to navigate the volume of memories I recovered if it weren't for her guidance.

I'd also like to thank my girls. They remind me every day of what truly matters, right here and now, and just how spectacular life has become for me.

Finally, I'd like to thank Dr. Marguerite Pinard, MD. Her expertise in working out dosage requirements to treat the chemical imbalances my childhood traumas left in my head has not only helped me to thrive, but it truly saved my life. She has also reviewed the book at a couple stages of development and challenged me to fix portions of it, not grammatically, but by adjusting my views of certain situations.

Contents

Foreword

This is a true story of intense traumatic abuse and heartwarming inspiration. It is told by the man who lived it and not only survived, but through determination and perseverance, overcame almost impossible odds to create for himself a life that is meaningful, successful, and truly happy.

I am a clinical psychologist, one of the therapists Kevin consulted. I had the privilege of working with him as he valiantly struggled to understand and resolve the emotional pain, anxiety, anger, and rage he was experiencing as a result of his childhood trauma.

Around 2006, Kevin walked into my office for the first time. He was like most people on their first few visits. He knew he wanted to get better, but he was intimidated at the point he had reached—to find himself in my office. He fairly quickly relaxed and began to let go of some horrible memories. It didn't take long for me to realize he had more than a minor grievance with his mother, as he first had thought when he came in. Over the course of the next ten years, I helped him process and make sense of dozens of memories as they seemed to continuously roll in at times. As you'll read through his book, these memories ranged from mundane to a truly terrifying testimony on just how evil mankind can be.

Through the years, I had treated people who had been abused as badly and even worse than Kevin had been; however, I had never treated someone who had lived through such difficulties and come out to be what may appear to a lay person as unscathed. He should have become lost in alcoholism when he went out drinking with his friends in high school, if not earlier. He should have graduated to harder drugs that would ultimately kill him or cause further escalation of his rage that would end with him in prison, possibly on murder charges. Alternatively, he should have succumbed to his suicidal ideations. The degree of loneliness and isolation people suffering this amount and type of abuse is for all intents and purposes intolerable for nearly anybody. He should also have lashed out at authority figures, such as his teachers, and failed his classes rather than excelling in them. He should not have been capable of becoming all that he did professionally. In short, there were about one hundred mines in the road he traveled, laid by his family as he grew up. Any one of them would have been fatal if hit. He brushed against a couple, but never hit any square. I wanted to know "how?"

Through the past thirty-five-plus years, I have guided numerous patients through absorbing recovered memories. I have learned to discern memories that are not necessarily based on fact versus those that are likely to be later corroborated by other means. Some things about Kevin's memories that stand out to me include the way they came in disjointed, out of order. He would speculate on how they would fit together during a session. At some later session, he would often come in to tell me his assumption was way off, then tell me how the previous fragments actually fit together. I don't think his assumed versions were correct even once. Every time it looked like a memory would take a straight path, it took a sudden curve. Additionally, he shared many of the less or non-traumatic memories with his brother, including one from when he was only about five years old. His brother verified having an identical or nearly identical memory to many of those recovered memories. You can't routinely fabricate identical memories in two different people. His routine recovery of memories that could be readily corroborated lends a lot of credibility to the ones for which no one else is still alive to corroborate. Above that, his most traumatic memory has very convincing corroborating coincidences associated with it.

I provided a first cut on editing his book. I've read it from cover to cover and can honestly say I was there when many of these memories came back to him. I saw and felt his pain, and his anger, as he related the memory to another person for the first time. I met his father at one of our sessions. It would have been around the 2008/2009 timeframe when Kevin quotes some of his more supportive, helpful emails. It was a stunning session. His father turned, rather ruthlessly, on Kevin. He accused him of being a horrible child who he and his wife had to work tirelessly to keep under control. Fortunately, I had been working with Kevin on a weekly basis for years by that time. I knew Kevin very well. I knew his father was undeniably lying. I could see it not only in his words but in his body language. Kevin and I brainstormed the next week to try to determine what in the world had happened the previous week. With additional years of new memories and new revelations from his father, it seemed clear his father was threatened by Kevin's attempts to get help to unlock his past. It appears that his father wanted me to look at Kevin with suspicion, and he wanted to confuse and throw Kevin himself off the path. He didn't want the truth—that he, like his father before him, was a horribly evil man—to come out.

I'm proud of Kevin's ability to think so critically, clearly, and especially deeply about these memories and their implications on his life. He has never been one to hide from difficult and painful memories. Every time he saw a thread of memory, no matter how much it hurt, he had to know what it was attached to. He had an unstoppable drive to determine what exactly it was that made him who he was. Even so, to have reached the point where he can pull it all together in such detail, to be able to reach out to others with this story in the hope of helping someone else, is a commendable step and truly exciting to see.

That being said, there are some things I'd like to caveat about his conclusions. When he approached me to review the book, he asked for an open and honest assessment of the presentation of the material—along with an honest assessment of his conclusions of how he succeeded as he did. I know he truly wants to do something positive for people, and the last thing he wants is to lead them down a dead-end road. I don't have any question that what he wrote in this book is exactly what worked for him. I grew to know Kevin very well, and I can see his personality in every step he describes in how he thrived. My concern is that this approach worked for Kevin. He was able to focus his anger and use it as a tool, for the most part. Even his "controlled" anger sometimes spilled out in inappropriate ways, though. He had a few fairly raucous arguments with his wife, Jill, through the years—despite his lifetime of self-training in handling this approach. Someone less well versed in redirecting the anger could have difficulty, especially without a psychologist helping them make sense of where the anger is coming from, so they can completely eliminate the lion's share of it rather than refocusing every bit of it. I think this is what Kevin is pushing for through his book, but I felt it was worth reiterating.

This approach, or a hybrid approach customized with your therapist, may be beneficial to you; however, I implore you, as Kevin did in his book, to please find a good psychologist—and don't simply rely on this approach because Kevin was able to make it work for him. As a reminder, too, it only worked for Kevin because he allowed more than a few people to help him make it. As Kevin has said, the mind is tremendously complex, and you're undoubtedly going to need tweaks in the approaches spelled out here, or maybe for you, nothing in this approach will work. You'll get much farther with help.

I encourage you to keep reading, though. I can almost guarantee that you will get something out of this book. It's a remarkable story of survival and conquest from someone who had the cards heavily stacked against him.

—Mary J. Watson, PhD

Introduction

My name is Kevin. To an outsider, it looks like I've lived a very normal, successful life. It's funny how, with a lifetime of practice, you can fool outsiders so easily.

I grew up through the 1980s in western New York in your typical house out in the suburbs. No white picket fence, but we did have a basketball hoop in the driveway. I had two parents, an older brother, and a cat. We tried to adopt a dog once, but my mother hated it, so that didn't last long. We also had a second cat for a while, but my mother traumatized it so badly that we had to give it away for its own good.

I went to public schools where I was always a straight-A student. I played the violin early, and the clarinet later, in elementary school. I earned the third chair in a statewide band competition when I was in sixth grade. I pretty much excelled at everything I did, except sports.

By late high school, I even turned the sports shortcoming around. I molded myself into a great weightlifter. In eleventh grade, I maxed around 315 pounds on bench and over 600 pounds on squats. My knees still hate me for that one. I did reasonably well in football and field events in track. In twelfth grade, I placed high in state competitions for shot put.

Don't worry, though; I wasn't all work and no play. My friends and I spent the better part of our weekends attempting to pound the most beers. My crowning party achievement came in eleventh grade. My friend and I bought a case of beer to split between us. He must have had a stomach bug of some sort, because he got sick after only three beers. That was certainly not his usual limit. I suddenly found myself on the receiving end of twenty-one beers. I polished off every one of them within the next four or five hours. I demanded that we buy more beer before the stores cut off sales. My friends said if I could walk a straight line, they would help me find someone to get more alcohol. They had no doubt that I wouldn't be able to do it after drinking twenty-one beers. I walked the straight line. Effortlessly. My friends were stunned, but equally concerned I could get hurt if I drank any more. Because of their concerns, they laughed it off and refused to help me get more.

I truly had the greatest friends anyone could ask for. They were a lot of fun to be around; but at the end of the day, we always looked out for each other—in the same way they made sure I didn't drink too much that one night. My two best friends, Dave and Bill, both smoked at least on occasion. I was a lot bigger than them, but they made sure I knew if I ever took up smoking, they would find a way to kick my ass. They never presumed that I wanted to follow in their footsteps when it came to substances. Whenever I needed to take a step away from drinking so much, they eagerly supported my decision, even if they fully intended to get obliterated themselves. We also shared a lot of common interests—ranging from blaring Metallica way too loudly to exploring the swamp Dave and I lived near—with our trusty hunting knives at the ready in case we were attacked by one of the wild dogs that lived there, according to the local myths. Then there were the epic, late-night Risk games. I don't know how, but it seemed like Dave whooped us every time. I always figured he'd end up as a military general later in life!

I was always painfully shy around girls. That finally changed in twelfth grade. I went to a heavy metal concert featuring Megadeth and Judas Priest with a group of friends. Some were friends of friends who I didn't know at all. At some point while Judas Priest was on stage, my friends and I were standing a bit outside the mosh pit. A fat guy who had to weigh well in excess of three hundred pounds very forcefully started shoving his way through the crowd, causing most of us to lose balance. I quickly regained my stance and gave an even harder shove back in the direction where the push had come from. The crowd parted like the Red Sea, leaving this bully and me staring each other down from about fifteen feet apart. He shouted some threat to me; I responded in a "try me" type of attitude. I didn't want to fight him. He had enough weight behind him that I would have been knocked into next week if he'd managed to land a punch. Also, I was afraid my right knuckle was broken because of a minor altercation I'd had with my friend over a floor hockey game earlier that week; however, I absolutely wasn't going to back down from this horse's ass, either. That sums up most of my life: don't go looking for trouble, but sure as hell don't run from it like a coward either. We stared each other down with fists clenched for what felt like hours. Eventually, he slowly turned and disappeared into the crowd. I did the same.

I didn't know until about a week later, but one of the girls in the group of friends had noticed me even before the altercation. Our friends managed to get us alone together, and we ended up dating for about five years, becoming very good friends in the process. Her take on me from that night, which I think sums me up as well as anyone could, was that I was clearly extremely angry at that guy. She said I looked so angry as I stared him down that she is certain my eyes were glowing red. Unlike any other guy or girl she had known to that point, however, I was willing to walk away from the anger—rather than going in with all guns blazing and dealing with the consequences later. She loved the presence of that internal fire, combined with the mastery I showed over it in that circumstance.

In short, I was your typical kid who was very driven to get ahead of the field. At the same time, I drank heavily to drown out a lot of pain that fueled the red-hot rage burning inside me with a fury that could make the sun weep with jealousy. People hear my drinking stories from high school and say, "Boy, you really knew how to party!" Sadly, no. I drank hard so I could survive.

They didn't see the abuse. They didn't see the horrifying memories my subconscious was working so hard to keep buried. I was a master of swallowing the pain and keeping it hidden from everyone. For the most part, I was even able to hide it from myself.

I continued on through school to earn two master's degrees. I later got married and have remained married for over twenty years. My wife and I have two daughters.

People now see a guy with two master's degrees in engineering, a wife of over twenty years, and two remarkably well-adjusted teenage daughters—and think I have always had all the answers. They couldn't be more wrong. I have spent months and years at a time extremely lost in the pain and loneliness of my upbringing. I spent decades finding the answers I needed to navigate my way out of the isolation.

Today, I'm that quiet guy at the party. Because of my apparent successes, people mistake that for arrogance. Not a chance. I'm friendly, but reserved. Happy to talk the latest tech advancement or college ball game, but more comfortable out by the firepit staring into the flames, escaping into my own thoughts somewhere far away.

People often wonder where I go while I'm in that zone. "What are you thinking about?" Sometimes I'm in the here and now: plotting our next move on how to secure, grow, and strengthen the business my wife, Jill, and I have worked so hard to build. Or sometimes I'm worrying about our girls. They're amazingly well-grounded but sometimes don't make the choices we would like them to make. Often, though, I'm contemplating how a parent could possibly hate their offspring as mine hated me, or I'm revisiting a young girl's horrifying screams from long ago, or contemplating whether or not I really brushed against death once, and if so, why I'm still here.

There's a lot I must explain for you to understand those thoughts. I hope in doing so, you may find some inspiration—inspiration to power through anything that tries to bring you down, inspiration to do more to lift others up, or inspiration for any other area in your life that needs it.

1

Background

IN THE SUMMER OF 1972, my parents already had a two-year-old son: my brother, Bryan. My mother, Mary Ellen, was pregnant with another baby, me, and due to give birth in October. Naturally, there weren't any scientific techniques readily available in 1972 to determine the gender of a baby, so my mother relied on tried and seemingly true wives' tale methods.

My mother was ecstatic to be expecting a girl. Her long-time dream had been to raise a daughter. She "knew" she was carrying a girl for many reasons. She had suffered through a lot of morning sickness with Bryan. There was almost no morning sickness with me. She had carried Bryan low in her belly, but this baby was carrying high. They tried other tests, too, such as the ring test. All signs pointed toward a girl!

Numerous friends and family tried to warn my mother not to get too fixated on the results of the wives' tale methods, but she was almost desperate for a daughter and wouldn't hear of any possibility of carrying a boy. On October, Friday the thirteenth, 1972, that all came crashing down. Hard. I was born. A boy. My mother didn't believe the doctor when he told her I was a boy, but he was right.

Later that evening, her husband—my dad, Ron—could clearly see how depressed she was.

"We could try a third time for a girl!" he offered, trying to give her some hope.

"I would KILL myself if I had a third boy," was her response.

It wasn't so much the words as the feeling behind the words. The hairs on the back of my dad's neck literally stood up—possibly for the first time in his life. Upon hearing the words and tone in her voice, he had no doubt in his mind: *she was serious.*

Bryan had been a colicky baby. His tantrums and fits were enough that my dad and mother almost didn't have any more children.

On the other hand, once I was born, I seemed to be straight out of a 1950s-era propaganda skit about how ideal home life should be, according to my father's recollections.

Of course, my mother didn't see it that way.

Following my rough introduction to this world, when I was three years old, my parents decided to move from Rochester, New York, to a relatively small suburb named Penfield. They felt my brother and I would have a better chance for a good education there. Penfield was known in the area for having one of the best public-school systems around; city schools didn't rate quite as high.

My father's parents owned some land along a relatively remote road in Penfield, so my father purchased a piece of that property for very cheap and had a house built on it. It was a fairly large plot of land, for the suburbs—probably a half-acre or larger. Our house was on a public water supply, but we had a septic tank for the sewage. The tank was pretty much right in the middle of our large backyard. In part because of the tank, the backyard was left wide open, making a perfect playing field for Bryan and me. Bryan was two and a half years older, so I had to learn early how to handle some very hard throws from a stronger arm. We spent more time throwing the football around back there than anything else. We both made our share of amazing circus catches, and even more embarrassing drops. The deeper the snowdrifts, the better, as far as we were concerned when it came to tossing the ball around. The games of "kill the carrier" were epic when we could gather enough friends.

Standing at the back of the house looking out, my father had planted a hedgerow to the left that defined that property boundary. To the right was a natural drainage ditch with some large trees and overgrown bushes. A short, old, stone wall covered with a canopy from the overgrown bushes and trees ran near the middle of that drainage ditch. As a younger kid, I spent hours exploring that old wall—fantasizing about who may have built it, when they did, and why.

A swamp named "The Thousand-Acre Swamp" took over where my backyard ended. I don't know if it was really a full one thousand acres as named, but as deeply as we trekked into it at times, we never did find the other end. The stone wall mysteriously continued one hundred yards or deeper into the swamp.

My father built a stone wall of his own along the front border of the property, with another hedgerow behind the wall. I vaguely remember "helping" build the wall, but I was still very young at the time.

Looking from the road, a large black walnut tree grew alongside the house. I remember it as a big tree then, and as far as I know, it is still there. We once watched a neighborhood cat toying with a chipmunk it had caught in the front yard. We looked on helplessly from the family room window, as the cat allowed the apparently injured chipmunk to hobble just so close to the tree before pouncing on it and dropping it a little farther away. This went on for some time, as the chipmunk slowly inched its way closer and closer to the tree. Then, like a flash, the chipmunk shot to and up the tree, leaving the cat dumbfounded over what in the world had just happened. This "helpless" chipmunk shocked the cat with its resiliency and guile. The cat had every advantage, but the chipmunk beat it. We had a good laugh at the cat's expense.

Beyond the black walnut tree was a large open field with a big red barn at the other end. When we first moved into the house, this field was owned by a gentleman I only knew as Mr. Moore. The field was fenced off, and two brown horses lived there. Somehow it was brought to my attention that I could feed the horses by pulling up a fistful of the long grass growing along the fence and reaching my arm up over the fence to offer them the treat. The horses grew to trust me and would readily come when they saw me gathering up grass. When I was in kindergarten or first grade, I was spending some time alone with the horses when a photographer for the local paper happened to be driving by. She snapped a picture that led to my fifteen minutes of fame among all my classmates. The day after the picture ran, nearly all my classmates showed me the pictures their moms had snipped from the paper—amazed that I was featured in such a large picture in the paper.

The house had a two-car garage. A concrete walkway led from the driveway to the front door, set back slightly from the garage. When I was still very young, my father added a two-car turnaround. With the natural build-up of winter snow, and the snow my father blew off the driveway, huge mounds of snow accumulated in the corners of the turnaround and driveway. My brother would dig a trench into one of the banks, I would dig a trench into the other, and we would have one heck of a snowball fight. One year, we had a once-in-a-lifetime event. We simultaneously stood up from behind our walls and let our snowballs fly. Midway across the driveway, the snowballs hit. Dead center. It wasn't a glancing blow that sent them off course. They were mutually annihilated. We screamed in delight and disbelief, then spent hours trying to recreate the event. We eventually gave up. At some point, my dad installed a basketball pole off the turnaround. Bryan and I spent probably years-worth of collective time playing one-on-one, horse, and other games at that hoop. Sadly, I still can't hit the broad side of a barn if I throw a basketball at it. I still have fun trying, though.

We almost exclusively used the garage to enter the house. Through most of my childhood, we only had one car. My mother was a stay-at-home mom, and my father drove the car back and forth to work. They would typically grocery shop and run other errands on the weekends. My father parked in the farthest, leftmost bay of the garage. Makeshift racks hung from the ceiling, full of miscellaneous "spare parts" from whatever accumulated over time. In the right bay was a large snow blower, which was pretty much required when living this close to Lake Ontario. Bryan and I typically kept our bikes in this bay as well. It wasn't a good idea to leave them in the wrong bay, even momentarily. I learned that lesson well when I was five, which I'll get into later. An assortment of other miscellaneous tools, fertilizers, and equipment filled the rest of the bay.

The garage was attached to the main house through a door, which opened into a very small hallway. My father cut out a door in the wall facing the garage door to add a kitchen pantry. The builder had closed off a good-sized area behind that wall, and my father was able to determine he could put that dead space to use. A scientist by education, he was very bright and clearly passed along his knowledge of math, engineering, and sciences to Bryan and me. Bryan later followed in his footsteps to become a chemist.

On one side of this small hallway was a half bath, and on the other end was the kitchen. The kitchen had an island. A peninsula separated the kitchen from what we used as the dining room. The kitchen sink faced the outside wall with a window over it, overlooking the backyard. My mother prepared great, home-cooked meals in that kitchen nearly every night.

The basement door also opened into the kitchen.

We typically ate our meals in the dining room adjacent to the kitchen, except on a big occasion when we would eat somewhere else—like going out for a burger or fish fry at Bill Grey's. For our birthdays, we would often choose somewhere like the local restaurant, Waldron's, just down the road from Abbott's Frozen Custard near the Webster Movie Theater. Yes, Abbott's was usually part of those outings!

The dining room of our house was also usually my father's sanctuary. Along the wall that separated the garage from the dining room was a set of shelves. Dad had an old reel-to-reel tape recorder that always fascinated my brother and me, but I don't think I ever actually saw it in use. A full set of *Encyclopedia Britannica* books lined up along one of the shelves. (For the younger readers, this was the old-fashioned version of a Google search.) Some other decorative items and a TV sat on the shelves.

My dad would spend most of his evenings sitting at the dining room table, playing solitaire and watching old movies on the TV. Occasionally, we'd get together to play a game as a family. Our game of choice was typically one my father called Chessinda. It was on a large piece of plywood my father had carefully framed, painted, and shellacked. The board and game play were pretty much identical to a more common board game called Parcheesi, and also similar to Sorry. This was a perfect game when a younger player, me, was involved. My mother would typically get angry and storm off after my father would send one of her pieces back to start. The three of us would continue and have a good time. It got to the point where my mother just wouldn't even begin a game, leaving it to the three of us to have fun.

The basement was half finished. The builder was supposed to leave it unfinished but proceeded about halfway through the process of finishing it before my parents noticed what he was doing. Instead of the bare cinderblock walls most basements had from floor to ceiling, the basement was lined with unfinished sheetrock. The rest looked like a standard basement. A dark red, metal support beam stood roughly in its center. Above, the floor joists, wiring, and ductwork were all visible. As a younger kid, I didn't have any trouble walking down there, but as I got older, I had to be careful where I stood upright, or I could whack my head pretty good. The floor was bare concrete, and the stairs to the main level were bare wood, painted a dark grayish-blueish color.

The stairs had a very recognizable creak when anyone walked on them. My father's shoes, in particular, left a very distinctive hollow thud on the stairs. For years, I had recurring nightmares in which I would hear his shoes, very slowly clumping one at a time up the stairs—slowly getting closer and closer to the top. I was always in the family room.

I was desperately trying to get behind something to hide. Other kids with me were already behind things—hiding, encouraging me on—but I could never squeeze through to reach them. I was too fat. Then, the doorknob rattled as my father grabbed it. The terror of that sound woke me in sheer panic every time. I was in high school before I lost a lot of weight, was able to slip safely behind a chair in the nightmare, and managed to permanently lay that horrible dream to rest.

Before those nightmares started, when I was very young, I learned how to control my dreams—to a certain extent. I could, in a way, become aware that I was in a dream. I would wake myself up just enough to gain better awareness of my surroundings, without ending the dream. My favorite thing to do once I rejoined the dream was to fly. It was exhilarating. Then one day, I lost control of the dream while flying. I went into a free-fall and couldn't recover control. I woke up in a panic. I tried to grab control of a couple dreams after that, but could never really get off the ground again.

My parents kept a fair amount of junk in the basement, including a dresser full of drop cloths and a bunch of very old records and 45s. Bryan and I would sometimes use the large open areas in the basement along with the materials available to make some amazing sheet forts. They were really more like sheet mansions, if you ask me. When I was little, I would also use an old chalkboard down there to play school by myself. Bryan was too cool to participate with me in that.

Back in the kitchen, in the opposite direction from the room we actually used as a dining room, was the room that the builder intended to be the dining room. We used it as more of a miscellaneous room—and never a dining room. For some time, we played video games there. I was a video game junkie. As part of the Atari 2600 generation, I would spend hours playing a variety of games. One of my favorites was Adventure—a game wherein I could slay three dragons, then basically play house in one of the castles. The graphics were comically rudimentary. My character was a square dot, for instance. In my head, I always saw more than just the simplistic lines; instead, I saw an entirely different life from the one I was living. Somewhere where I was in control. Somewhere where I was safe. I could go into the white castle, where I could only get to the back area of the castle by passing through an impenetrable wall with an object they referred to as a bridge in the game. It really was more of a "magical bridge" that allowed the user to pass over chasms or through walls. There was only one bridge in the game, so once I passed through the wall, I could grab the other side of the portable, magical bridge and drag it behind the wall with me, ensuring I was safe from everyone. I felt safer just fantasizing that was me, locked behind a wall no one could get through, because only I had access to the bridge. Higher scores for me weren't so much a way to exert dominance, although that was admittedly part of it; but the better my score, the longer it meant I could stay somewhere different.

Every Christmas, the miscellaneous room was used for the tree. It was always the easiest place to put it with minimal impact on the rest of the house. My mother typically almost seemed to enjoy putting me down and insulting me most of the year. Given that she didn't deride me as much as usual through December, leaving mostly good memories of Christmas, I've struggled for years trying to figure out why I still, to this day, get so angry and hurt as the holiday approaches. I even had my own ornament on the Christmas tree—the Little Drummer Boy. Looking back, I find it fitting that a symbol of someone who sees himself as worthless and devoid of anything to offer would be my Christmas ornament. I still look forward to hearing Bob Seger's version of the song every Christmas.

There were certainly moments when Christmas wasn't as idyllic as it could have been. One year, my brother and I pooled our money and got my father something we thought he would really like. His response? "Hmm." That was it. Just "hmm." I think I was sufficiently emotionally dead by that time in my life, so his reaction really didn't even register with me. It was just *Dad being Dad*.

Bryan, however, had had enough. He sarcastically exclaimed to the family, "He likes it! He really, really likes it! You know how I can tell?? Because he only gets that excited about something if he's REALLY mad, or if he's REALLY happy! He doesn't look mad, does he?! So he MUST love it!" Mind you, Bryan was the suck-up. He didn't mouth off. Ever. For him to reach enough of a limit to go off on an authority figure was really saying something. Neither my mother nor father had any kind of comeback for what he had said. Not even to scold him for saying something "inappropriate." They both knew he hit the nail on the head with that comment.

This situation still doesn't explain my current hatred/fear of Christmas, though. I find that memory to be quite amusing, actually.

When I was in college, the miscellaneous room was converted into a pseudo hospital room for my ailing grandmother. My father's father had recently shot himself, so the story goes, which will be covered in detail later, and my dad's mother was quickly reaching the end of her life due to complications from diabetes. Due to her health, she came to live with us.

During her stay, I unintentionally interrupted a phone call my grandmother and mother had received. My grandmother was in tears, although it seemed to me they were not genuine tears, saying over and over, "What an evil man." She noticed that I had walked into the room and was hesitantly looking at her and my mother. My grandmother shot me a look that quite honestly made my heart stop for a second— and pierced straight into my soul with such hatred that I knew it was clearly directed at me. I quickly exited to another room where I convinced myself to shake it off. Over the years, I became convinced my grandmother had just talked with my cousin or my cousin's mother for reasons you'll read in this book, and without saying a word, told me to, "Just shut the fuck up, or you'll regret it." More recent developments have put into question who they had been talking to.

The family room was attached to the "miscellaneous room." The two rooms were essentially one large, open room. The family room also directly opened to the kitchen. The family room window looked out to the front yard. You could see both the black walnut tree and the driveway from this window. Entering the room through the open door from the kitchen would lead to the foyer—and the stairs leading upstairs in just a few paces. The foyer was very small, maybe 5 by 5 feet in size. The stairs were partially open to the family room by a half wall. As a young kid, I loved to slide my GI Joe figures down the wooden cap that topped off the half wall. My mother was not too fond of that though, as she preferred I remain in my room, out of sight. Staying in my room was fine; there were always plenty of adventures I could concoct in there for my war figures.

At the top of the stairs was a hallway that ran both to the left and right. Going left would lead to my parents' room. I helped my dad re-paint this room while the Buffalo Bills' playoff game blared on the radio. This was the day Frank Reich brought the Bills back from something like a 45-point deficit to win the game. It's one of the few times I actually enjoyed painting—and one of the few times I really felt connected to my father in any meaningful way.

Toward the front of the house upstairs was the one bathroom all four of us shared: one sink, one toilet, and one shower. At the back of the house was a spare bedroom, which was also used as an office, but most often as a junk room.

Bryan's bedroom, also off the upstairs hallway, was really nice. It was large enough that he ended up with one of my parents', old, king-sized beds. He still had enough room for what we thought at the time was a pretty nice stereo—and a desk and dresser. The real kicker to me as a kid was that he had not one, but two windows. The only other room in the house with that kind of setup was the master! He also had a large closet. He was always quick to fire back by pointing out that the closet was mostly full of Mom's and Dad's stuff.

Since he had tunes and a great place to lay out and play games, his room was our routine meeting spot. I could probably count on one hand the number of times we did anything together in my room. We played our fair share of board games and a role-playing game called Star Frontiers in his room. Star Frontiers was a lot like Dungeons and Dragons, but much simpler in the respect that there weren't ten thousand different spells for wizards and other odd-ball things like that. Just a variety of laser guns and rifles and spaceships to fly. In other words, you could casually play it and didn't need a degree in all its ins and outs. We listened to a lot of music like Billy Joel and comedy records like Steve Martin on his stereo. As I got older, he introduced me to exercise routines, which evolved into a pseudo competition between the two of us to see who could lift the most weights. He had two years on me, so it was never a legitimate competition. Every time I took a couple steps forward, I would only catch where he had been a year or two before. I kept pushing forward with lifting, though.

A psychologist I saw for many years theorized that my brother and I were so heavily involved in weightlifting because events at our grandparents' house when we were very young left us with a subconscious need to feel capable of overpowering nearly anybody who might try to attack us. I never enjoyed playing most sports. For me, even consciously, lifting weights was always much more about preventing people from messing with me than about gaining strength to throw them around on the football field or seeking out fights with anyone. So I think my therapist could very well have been onto something with her hypothesis. Through high school, I played football, wrestled, or threw shot-put and discus, but I never really cared about any of them. I only cared about getting bigger and stronger to keep would-be attackers away.

Finally, in the grand tour of my childhood home, was my room. My sanctuary. It wasn't much, but it was mine. My window overlooked the backyard. I loved that. During summer nights, I could look out at the moonlit yard and listen to animals in the woods breaking branches or rustling leaves as they hunted for a nighttime meal. It was usually quiet enough that I could hear the crackle of gravel under car tires slowly navigating a driveway at my friend's house a good half-mile away. Outside my window and to the right was a fairly large tree—a good ten feet taller than the house, with one thick limb that reached out toward our backyard. My ever-loving brother convinced me when I was little that it was the Poltergeist tree, after we watched the original movie in the theater. In the movie, a tree outside a young boy's room comes to life during a fierce thunderstorm. It reaches into his room and nearly eats the boy before his father can reach him and save him from certain death. Bryan had two twin beds in his room at the time and wondered why he woke up the next morning to find me sleeping in his other bed! You've got to love big brothers!

My room. The place where Legos became a gateway to a new world. Not because my creativity took me there, but because my need to remain sane demanded that I go there. My room. The place I would wake in the middle of the night to find my restless dreams had prompted me to walk around in my sleep again. My room. The place where I'd wake from nightmares so terrifying that I couldn't even move or call out for help. My room. The place where I'd physically hurt myself to keep the emotional pain in check. My room. The first place where I was really able to sit down and contemplate what those suicidal thoughts were all about. My room. The place of nightmares.

Before we get more deeply into what I've discovered and how I think my revelations may help you, let me first give you greater details about my childhood.

CHAPTER

2

Early Childhood

FROM THE DAY I WAS BORN, my mother was disappointed in me. I easily angered her, and she frequently ignored me. Whether it was my existence as a boy instead of a girl—or the fact that she was already stressed out when I was born with a toddler under foot—it became clear that I was the brunt of her discontent.

Bryan, on the other hand, was the apple of her eye. She evidently always took good care of my brother, despite her distaste for me.

My dad found concern in how my mother treated me, to the extent that he found her behavior toward me to be abusive, even under his watchful eye. He feared for my welfare at her hands. It's unclear whether or not she would physically harm me, but from what I've been able to dig out of that era, she seemed more than capable of doing so emotionally. The stress of raising an infant and toddler could easily have put her over the edge.

When I was a toddler, my dad had an affair. He was on the verge of divorcing my mother. Her negative attitude toward me had extended onto him as well. My dad was sick of fighting with her over her treatment of both him and me, according to the recollection of one of my aunts who occasionally spoke with my father about my mother's behavior. By some accounts, my dad had gone as far as drawing up divorce papers. He changed his mind at the last minute, though. It came to his attention that under New York state law, he would lose all rights to Bryan and me if he filed for divorce.

My father's concern over my mother's treatment of me had its limits, however. My parents were seemingly well suited for each other. My father, by his own admission had been raised in an extremely abusive home. Physical, sexual, and emotional abuse ran rampant. The abuse even included threats from his father to kill him and his siblings—a dynamic that would be spotlighted as I got to know my grandfather. My father had been so immersed in this way of life, he in turn abused his younger siblings.

So at times, it was my mother who played protector.

One of my earliest memories comes from when I was five. My father came home from the grocery store. He was irate because either Bryan or I had left a bike in his car's garage bay when we came inside. Bryan and I had just sat down to eat lunch at the peninsula between the dining room and kitchen. My mother was standing in the kitchen when my dad came in yelling and fuming over the egregious act. It escalated from there. He brought a gallon jug of milk in from the car. Back in 1978, plastic gallon milk jugs were designed to be much stronger than they are by today's standards. My father slammed the jug on the island. Despite the container's strength, the jug exploded milk and shrapnel throughout the kitchen.

To my father, this was normal behavior.

To my mother, however, this was unacceptable. She calmly told Bryan and me, "Go to your rooms. You're not in trouble. I just need you to go to your rooms right now." She physically put herself between us and my father as soon as she could get into position. I stopped halfway through the family room, peering through the kitchen door. I could see the back of my mother's head and my father's angry face scowling at me from beyond. He stared at me and motioned with his head in an upward jerk, indicating to my mother that someone was behind her. My mother turned around and repeated, "I need you to go upstairs right now. You're not in trouble, and I'll get you when I'm done here." I agreed. Before I left, I could see my mother turning back around. Her face mutated from a calm appearance to the look of a lion about to leap onto its prey. I don't remember what I did or did not hear from their altercation, but I do know that my father never blew up like that again. Whatever my mother said, it must have been extraordinarily persuasive.

I think this memory really stood out, even at such an early age, for two reasons. First, it was the first time I felt truly physically threatened. The way my father looked at my brother and me while raging was terrifying. Second, this was one of only two times in my life that I felt protected, loved, and/or supported by my mother. As far as I know, this was the first time she stood up for me in any way—and it was in a huge way. I cling to this memory as one of only a few truly *precious* memories in my childhood.

The next couple years came and went largely as the others. Until my father's plan to leave us at the mercy of his father took shape in the summer of 1980.

CHAPTER

3

The Summer of 1980

WE WOKE UP to a beautiful western New York summer morning. It was 1980. I was seven and Bryan was barely ten. As usual, the sun was shining bright, the temperature was warm but not yet hot, and there was that perfect summer smell in the air. My brother and I were spending two weeks with my grandparents. We were very excited to be down at their remote house in the farmlands of Avon. There were plenty of wide-open places to run and more important to me, an Atari 2600 with tons of games and nobody telling me I had spent enough time on it for one day!

My grandmother was a very active woman. She left the house shortly after sunrise and rarely got back home much before sunset. They only had one car, and she used it most of the day. In western New York, that meant she was gone running errands for nearly twelve hours during the summer months. I don't think there was a farmer's market or relative she didn't spend hours with during any given month through the summer.

My grandfather also kept very busy. He spent the vast majority of his time working in the garage—repairing equipment, tearing out hedges in the yard, working in their large vegetable garden, or puttering on something else. He rarely left the property. He always seemed to have a cigarette in one hand and a bottle of beer in the other. Oddly, he never appeared to be drunk or buzzed and never seemed to suffer any ill effects from the cigarettes. He was rather gruff around me, seemingly uncomfortable around kids. Or perhaps he just hated them.

This day didn't seem any different than the others. My grandmother was getting ready to leave.

"Do you want to go with me?" my grandmother said, inviting my brother and me to join her.

As usual, my brother eagerly joined her.

I preferred to stay home and play on the Atari. To me, there wasn't anything worse than being cooped up in a car driving to the ends of the Earth for hours on end—or at least I thought there wasn't.

The events that unfolded over the next few hours would define who I was to become in life. These few hours spawned much of the hatred, loneliness, terror, pain, and dread that have plagued me for decades. I still have nightmares about that day. I would go years at a time without a good night's sleep because of those nightmares.

My first flash of memory about the events of this summer came when I was still in high school. It didn't strike me as anything important when it first came to mind, but I saw my grandfather in the door that led from the family room out to his back room. I could only see him from his stomach up. A reclining chair covered everything below his stomach.

Two things always disturbed me in the memory, even as far back as high school.

First and foremost was his look. The stare. He was staring at me in such a cold, angry, dark way that I can't put a name to it.

Second was a grunt. I couldn't quite place it back in high school. It took me almost five years before out of the blue it hit me.

Shortly after my grandfather died in 1992, my father pulled me aside one night. He told me much of what I now know about my grandfather's past and my cousin's run-in with him, all of which I'll describe later.

But then he asked me a question in a rare moment of transparency that seemed quite odd. "Did Grandpa ever…?"

I don't think I even let him finish getting the question out before I extremely defensively shot a quick "no." I somehow knew he was asking if my grandfather had ever molested me.

As soon as I began voicing the response, I was stunned by the veracity of my defensiveness. Almost immediately, the vision of my grandfather in the doorway began coming more often and more clearly. It wasn't long after my father's question when it came clearly enough to realize what he was doing, and to realize the grunt I'd heard in my vision was him having an orgasm.

Sometime early in college, I began uncovering a memory of talking with my brother late at night about staying at the house during the day—instead of going with him and Grandma to run errands. I started piecing things together, somewhat. The incident with my grandfather staring at me while masturbating had occurred because I chose to stay home alone with him while Bryan and Grandma left for the day to run errands.

In my memory, Bryan began making an argument for why I should go with them the next day. "Grandma was really sad you didn't come with…," he said.

I didn't even let him finish. I interrupted him with, "I'll go with you tomorrow." I assumed this abrupt change in my decision of where to spend my day came in response to my grandfather masturbating in the doorway. But I'd later remember I was alone with my grandfather more often than that one time, so the conversation with my brother must have come at a later date. Perhaps this memory came before nearly any others to tell my conscious mind that everything ended reasonably well.

I eventually found a way to protect myself. Unfortunately, I found it too late.

The memories of that summer stopped coming for a very long time. I would get minor "feelings" about events, but nothing clear—and nothing to fill in the big picture. I assumed the memories were done. But I could not have been more wrong. The worst were yet to come.

4

Adolescence

MY FUZZY AND DISTURBING INTERACTIONS with my grandfather didn't change my relationship at all with my mother. She remained an abrasive person to both me and others. I'm not sure if my mother actually liked anyone outside a tight group of friends and relatives. She would pretend to be everyone's best friend, then deride them on the ride home about any miscellaneous thing they may have done or said.

Throughout my adolescence, I believe my mother was genuinely destructive and trying to hurt me. Her "attacks" would include chastising me for everything she could, including getting anything less than 100 percent on tests. This happened even if I only missed one question.

I would hand my mother the test.

"Oh, wow. Ninety-five percent!" she would say, feigning excitement. Her pleased face transformed into that of half exasperation, half anger as she scanned through the test.

"Look here!" she demanded, pointing at the question I answered wrong. She handed the test back to me as she demanded, "Read back through that question!" She would wait a few seconds until I nodded that I had read it.

"It's the easiest question on the test! How could you get that one, out of all the others, wrong?!"

I shrugged my shoulders and quietly and full of shame replied, "I don't know."

"Well I know. It's because you're *lazy*! You're never going to be anything but a failure, because you're too *lazy* to make anything of yourself! If you had taken the time you should have on this test, you would have answered that question correctly!"

You may think it turned the tables when I got 100 percent on a test, which I frequently did. Not at all. She would go through roughly the same scenario, but in the end conclude with, "This just goes to show how *lazy* you are! Last week, you only got 95 percent, when this test proves you are capable of getting 100 percent all the time! You're going to be *nothing but a failure*, because you refuse to put the proper time in on anything."

Mind you, I was a straight-A student in every subject throughout elementary and middle schools. As a result of her put-downs, I always tried as hard as I could to get 100 percent.

No matter what I did, I was accused multiple times per day of being *lazy, stupid, disappointing*, and just downright *worthless*. In early childhood, I just absorbed the abuse. By adolescence, I began to learn how to fight.

I strove to be as evil and hateful as I could to my enemies through middle and high school. My theory was: *if you're the meanest person in the room with an intelligent approach, you're untouchable.* In every movie or fairy tale, this was true.

Yes, fairy tales would end with the evil person defeated, but everyone knew that the weak, fragile victor, in reality, could never overcome the hatred of their tormentor. Nor could the victor overcome the strength the villain built through that hatred.

No matter how strong, a person had to pick their battles. *You can only extend yourself so far,* I'd remind myself. Satan himself drew the line at an all-out altercation with God.

During my adolescence, I sharpened my adversarial skills through one confrontation after another with my mother. *Satan incarnate.* My ultimate goal was to be more hateful and aggressive than my mother.

I was unaware of it at the time, but I was also driven by another, deeper need—a villain with a more hidden and more powerful role: my grandfather. This character was behind the scenes, driving my unconscious behavior in ways I didn't yet see.

In seventh grade, I had very low self-esteem and typically didn't stick up for myself. Other kids on the bus noticed that and fairly mercilessly picked on the big, quiet kid. I put a stop to it one day. It was winter, and the two girls who were the ring leaders of the teasing smuggled snowballs on the bus. They were throwing what by then had become small ice balls at the back of my head. I tolerated it, because they were girls—and I didn't know what else to do. When a boy named Chris decided he'd start throwing some ice balls, I knew exactly how to handle that situation. I charged him as soon as the ice ball left his hand. He was significantly smaller than me and ducked down in a defensive posture. I began berating his face with a series of uppercuts. As I hacked at his face, I stared eye to eye with the taller, more powerful of the two girls. She responded by throwing an ice ball that happened to hit me directly in my eye. I didn't even blink or look away. I continued to stare her down while throwing punches at Chris and watching crystals of ice drip over my eyeball and past my pupil. She slowly dropped eye contact and looked down at the floor. She continued almost slowly melting—until she was sitting in her seat, hunched over, looking at the floor.

"What's wrong?" her friend asked.

She just shook her head quickly and muttered something. Her friend sat down beside her.

Nobody really ever picked on me much again after that, and that was the last fight I got into. I picked up that people would occasionally talk behind my back, but nobody was brave enough to face me—not even once I got into high school. The girl I stared down never looked me in the eye again. We went to the same high school after that, and when she'd see me coming, she would move as far to the other side of the hallway as she could—and keep her eyes averted.

I've been told I have a very frightening stare when I'm mad. That fight was apparently the first public display of my "enraged look"—and shows that fights with my mother had already honed my skills enough to give birth to a stare that could melt the toughest of bullies.

In fights with my mother, I would emotionally push back at least a little every time she emotionally pushed me. By eighth grade, this erupted into a full-scale war.

Late in the winter, my parents were washing dishes in the kitchen one evening after dinner. I had finished all my homework and was sitting in the adjacent family room watching TV, relaxing a bit before heading off to bed. My mother yelled into the family room, "Kevin! Go get the clothes out of the dryer!"

We had a relatively small house with the washer and dryer down in the half-finished basement to preserve living space. As a fourteen- or fifteen-year-old teenager should, I grumbled my way into the kitchen where the basement door was located, and headed down the creaky stairs into the cold, musty basement.

The dehumidifier hummed away quietly in the corner over near the sump pump. I pulled the dryer door down. It was one of the top-down doors, forming something of a ledge when open. It was a full load, and I didn't have a hand available to close the dryer door, so I bumped the door with my foot. That action slammed the door shut due to its common, spring-loaded mechanism.

When I got upstairs, you would have thought my mother just heard me fire the shot that killed Kennedy.

"Why did you slam the dryer door?!" she yelled at me.

"I DIDN'T!" I shot back.

"I have ears, you know! I heard it slam!" she returned.

I went on to try to explain how the spring mechanism works on the dryer door. She was unimpressed. I dropped the load of laundry in a chair and could hear and feel the rumble of the floor as she stomped her way toward me. I turned around just in time to see her nose to nose with me—and to block her first slap.

As accustomed as she was to being emotionally abusive, she couldn't throw a punch to save her life. She could never really hurt me, other than when I was a younger child and she spanked me with a large wooden spoon, so I never really considered her physically abusive. She certainly was not physically abusive in the sense that a man is often depicted physically abusing his children, but I guess when it really comes down to it, she very much would have been had she been physically capable of it.

I was old enough and big enough at this point that I didn't care how badly I pissed her off by blocking her punches.

In the past, I would have just let her hit me. Today, I just didn't care anymore.

She came at me with a series of rights and lefts. I blocked every single one of them. I can't remember exactly, but I think I may have even rolled my eyes at her while doing so.

She lost it. She bull-rushed me at that point. By eighth grade, I was taller and stronger than her, but she outweighed me by a good bit. Using her weight to its max, she managed to slam me fairly hard into the wall behind me. She then grabbed my shirt and started bouncing me off the wall, until my cotton sports team T-shirt was pretty much in tatters.

Nothing in this interaction hurt me physically, but it crossed a line. *This was way too far over the line this time,* I thought.

That was her first volley in our all-out war. My volley came a couple months later. I was supposed to read two books for a book report. It was Saturday, and the book report was due Monday. I hadn't even started the first book. I was a brilliant kid, and I knew I could pull this off with yet another A. Putting off reading two books until two days before the report was due just made it a little more interesting.

I knew my mother wouldn't see my approach as "interesting," so I told her I had already read one of the books. Truth be told, I didn't even have either book yet.

"I need to read a couple short books for a book report Monday. I've already read one, but I need another one today. Can you guys drop me off at the library on your way to the grocery store this morning?" I asked as my parents were preparing the grocery list.

"Sure. Can you have the book checked out by time we come back that way from the store?" my mother asked.

"Yeah. The teacher gave us a list of books to choose from, so it should be really easy to find the author and pick one out," I replied.

I picked out the two books I needed and met them in the parking lot.

"I grabbed a second book just in case the first one is really bad. I'm sure it'll be fine, but you never know!" I said to cover my reason for bringing out a second book.

"That's a really smart idea," my mother replied. "What book have you already read for the report?"

I told her the name of one of the other books from the list.

"Oh. How did you like it?" she asked.

"It was surprisingly good. I expected these books to be complete pretty-boy trash, but it was actually really good!" I responded, feeling pretty confident in how I was addressing her questions.

"Who were the main characters?" she pressed on.

I stammered a bit, kicking myself immediately for the obvious hesitation, then blurted out a couple names.

My mother was clearly onto me at this point. You could see the anger flaring up in her face. She quickly shot another question, trying to confirm her suspicions once again that I was nothing but a *lazy, good for nothing liar*. "What was the story about?"

I began rattling off an awkward plot, and almost as soon as I started, my mother turned nearly a completely impossible 180 in her seat and shouted directly in my face, "YOU DIDN'T READ THE BOOK! DID YOU?!"

I was caught. There was nothing I could do but come clean and point out that I had the short books ready, and this report would be nothing for me to whip off. My mother would hear none of it. She angrily turned to my father and shouted at him "Did you hear his lies?! It's all he ever does! He's nothing but a worthless liar! All you have to say about it is just to SIT there?!"

My father attempted to stammer something out, but she was back to facing me and barraging me with another set of insults.

The remainder of the five-mile drive home followed the same pattern. My father sat silently, presumably hoping she didn't turn to him again, all the while she reminded me over and over about what a lying, lazy, stupid, worthless piece of garbage I was.

It was springtime in western New York, so what started as a cold day had already significantly warmed. My dad parked the car in the driveway, and I got out with my books in hand. By time I reached the garage, my mother was right behind me—throwing right and left slaps at my back and the back of my head. I ignored her the best I could.

I proceeded into the house, entering the kitchen first. I set the books on one of the counters and started removing my jacket. My mother continued her physical assault the whole time. I walked through the family room, then into the foyer. My mother closely followed the entire time, hacking at me like she was trying to cut down a tree. I stood at the closet, hanging up my jacket. She continued her slaps. I turned, facing the wall with my back to her, reversing course back to the garage to help with the groceries. She continued to follow, slapping at my head, neck, and shoulders the entire time.

Halfway through the kitchen, something snapped. I stopped caring. Enough was enough. Consequences be damned. I stopped walking and began to swing my right arm as hard as I could in a circular swing in her direction.

By eighth grade, I was pushing 6 feet tall and probably about 170 pounds. I was not a small kid. I towered over my mother. Had I continued this "bitch slap" unimpeded, I may have truly hurt her. Fortunately, that voice of reason spoke up as I began my swing.

"What are you doing?! That's your mother! You CAN'T do that!!"

"Okay," I said back, "but I've gone this far. She knows what I'm about to do. If I stop now, she's going to *own* me, and she'll know it. Life will turn from hellish to unbearable."

In the split second when I had that thought, I also concluded I needed to give her a warning shot. Something that let her know *I'm bigger and stronger—and she had better watch herself around me from now on.* With that, I continued my swing but came to a complete stop just before I touched her cheek. Immediately after stopping and before she could react, I started moving my hand again and *very* slowly touched her cheek. I touched her about as gently as you would touch a newborn. What started as an effort to hurt her turned into the second volley of what was to become a brutal war in the years to come.

After touching her cheek, I began turning around to resume walking out to the garage. My dad was to my right, slightly in front of me, directly in the eye shot of where I was turning. I hadn't even considered his role in this. I could physically take my mother. My father, however…

Our eyes locked. He gave me a nearly imperceptible grin and nod, almost telepathically telling me to just keep walking. I did.

I practically danced across the garage when I reached it. Behind me I heard my mother shout in an almost guttural tone "HE… HIT… MEEEEEE!!!"

My father's nonchalant response was, "Well… what did you expect him to do?!"

It was the first time, and one of the only times, I remember having anyone take my side to help fight her. It felt amazing. For the first time in my life, I didn't feel alone. I took an ultimate stand and found I had someone on my side for once.

My mother's increasing physical assaults stopped that day. She never laid a hand on me again after that warning shot.

She did, however, take that situation as a signal that she needed to amplify her verbal assaults.

On my end, I accepted crushing her physical assaults as a very important victory. It showed me that she wasn't invincible. I felt empowered. If I could defeat her physically in a somewhat intelligent way (I did, after all, only give her a small hint of what I was capable of, without giving in to truly hurting her), then I could defeat her mentally.

I just have to learn to be more aggressive and meaner, so I thought.

When I was in ninth grade, a cat I grew up with named Tigger developed cancer. He was on the order of thirteen years old, and the vet recommended that we euthanize him. He said treatments would be extraordinarily difficult for such an old cat, and he would be unlikely to survive the treatment's brutality. Tigger was essentially my cat. If we were all sitting in the same room, he would immediately choose to sit in my lap. He also had his own meow for me, as he kneaded on my stomach before laying down.

This irritated my mother to no end. She reasoned that she fed him and cleaned his litter, so he should prefer her.

The day came to euthanize Tigger. My dad was going to take him to the vet that morning on his way to work. I was expected to get picked up by my friend and driven to school as if nothing were happening that morning. Tigger was curled up on my lap as I waited for my friend to pull into the driveway. It was all I could do to pick him up and set him on the floor when my friend arrived. I had to simply walk away. If I stopped to say goodbye to Tigger, I would have broken down in tears. If cats are capable of loving someone, then he was undoubtedly the first—and to that point only—living creature that loved me.

My friend and I would usually talk about things on our way to school. I couldn't that day. I'd never had to fight so hard to choke back tears. I learned how to do so very quickly, though. By time we reached the school, I was back to my normal self. We joked and laughed our way into the building like it was just another day.

The pain remained buried and forgotten about for many months or maybe even a full year. Out of the blue one evening, a coworker at my part-time job asked, "Do you have any pets?"

I told him, "We had a cat for a lot of years, but we had to put him to sleep a few months ago." I almost lost it right there. But I had to hold it together. There was no way I would ever live down breaking out in tears in the middle of Wegman's Supermarket!

I remembered how I'd buried the pain the first time, but I didn't want to lose the pain again like I had then. I needed to put it somewhere I could access, so I could let it out when I was ready to do so.

I buried it just deep enough to accomplish that. I'd think very fleetingly about it through the evening to make sure it didn't slip under too deep. Later that night after I had eaten dinner, showered, and gone to bed, I pulled it out of my memory. I proceeded to bawl like a baby for a few hours.

I have little doubt my mother enjoyed putting me through hell that morning when I held my cat for the last time. Her jealousy of my relationship with Tigger was well known in the house. I'm sure that jealousy was driven as much by her need to isolate and belittle me as by her need to be the favorite. It was contrary to her goals for me to have the affections of even an animal at my side to challenge her ranking of my worth.

Over the next few years, our exchanges grew increasingly more frequent—and over increasingly mundane things. They also grew more raucous. I lost all sense of normalcy. When she yelled at me, I would simply unload a torrent of hate and venom right back at her. This only served to escalate her, though. She seemed to take my return volleys as a sign that she needed to amp up her end of the fight.

The tension escalated in that manner for a few years. Her return hatred made me try that much harder with each fight to be more aggressive and more intimidating—to finally defeat her.

About halfway through twelfth grade, my father was out playing cards with some friends from work. My brother was at college, so it was just my mother and me alone together at home. These situations never ended well. This one ended particularly poorly.

I had been in a minor argument with a friend at school. We had played intramural floor hockey that day, and we were up against some of the kids from the actual hockey team. I was playing goalie, or at least I was standing in the goal as they ran up the score one slapshot after another. I was frustrated but recognized we were amateurs up against kids who actually knew what they were doing. My friend on the other hand took the loss pretty seriously. He specifically called out my terrible showing in goal. I was already frustrated, then getting called out like that put me over the top. Being the hotheaded eighteen-year-old boy that I was, I punched the steel outside door in the school locker room. Hard. Yes, it hurt. A lot.

That evening, I was getting ready to clean my contacts. I was sitting at the peninsula counter in our kitchen, facing our family room. My mother was sitting within view on a recliner in the family room. Something sparked an argument to start. Being alone with nothing but our hatred for each other to mitigate this argument, it quickly started to get very heated. I realized I was out of disinfectant and went upstairs to my bedroom to get more. I slammed the door on my armoire shut. It bounced back open. That intensified my irritation, so I slammed it shut again—and punched it for good measure. In a brilliant move, I of course used the same hand and set of knuckles I had already hurt that day.

I went back downstairs, trying to shake the pain out of my hand, looking periodically at my knuckle for any sign to indicate how bad the damage was. It was really just a show to sucker my mother into insulting me for hurting myself. I really didn't have a plan for what I'd do from there, but I somehow knew if she pulled at that thread, it would give the adrenaline rush I would really need to get this fight going to the next level. Throughout my life, she tended to get angry or irritated at me whenever I would hurt myself. As many things about her as there were that irritated me, her attacks on me when I was hurt or sick were among those that would get me the angriest.

She was predictably drawn in. She shouted, "Good! I hope you really hurt it bad!"

It worked. She bit. I had a surge of adrenaline the size of a tidal wave. I stared, or more accurately, scowled at her in the recliner as I pounded my fist, knuckle first, onto the countertop as hard as I could.

I shouted, "Me too! I hope I broke it!"

The counters were a cheap laminate with a pressboard body. I was an avid weightlifter at the time, and I suspect the counters had to be rattling and sounding like they were about to fall apart under the force of my punches.

Then there was the stare. I had five years to further perfect my angry stare from when I'd reduced the bully to a broken wreck on the bus. There were few times I could achieve the same degree of anger as when I stared down my mother at that moment.

The combination of my slamming fist and angry look was enough to shut her up. That was the first time I ever made her stop an attack.

She backed down. It had been a long-time goal of mine. It's what I had always wanted. *I beat her! I stopped Satan in her tracks!* Why did I feel so empty? I was downright distraught.

I knew I wasn't sad for her. I didn't feel bad that she wasn't mean enough to outdo me.

I did a lot of soul searching in the next few days. I realized that I had beat her at her own game. I didn't beat her by being *who I wanted to be*; I beat her by being *a more awful person than she was*.

I realized I hadn't thought things through. I didn't want to be who I had become.

That night, as I lay awake in bed, I thought about a lot of things. *I know I was born to be a good person. I'm genuinely an empathetic person. I almost always bend over backwards to try helping those around me before I take for myself. Being an even worse version of my mother doesn't fit. I don't want it. I can be strong in better ways.* That night I saw my trajectory, and it scared me. I repulsed myself.

As an adult, I felt for a long time that I had been fighting for decades to undo what I did to myself as a kid–making myself as angry and violent as my mother through my high school years. Knowing what I know now, however, it's clear that the root of a lot of my anger falls on my grandfather's—and therefore my father's—shoulders.

5

Life Beyond My Childhood Home

IN 1991, I GRADUATED FROM HIGH SCHOOL and moved off to college. It took me a couple years to decompress from full-time life with my parents and really start shedding some of the anxieties and self-doubts that weighed me down so tremendously. By my junior year, I began making some very good friends. I attended a school near Syracuse, so it was a fairly short bus trip back to Penfield to see my high-school girlfriend, Dawn, on most weekends.

My parents staunchly opposed me seeing Dawn. They didn't make any secret about how much they hated her and felt I should break up with her. The thing is, she was the first person I knew who was broken like me.

The truly odd thing is that I had no idea I was broken at the time. I had become so good at lying, even to myself, that I convinced myself I was "normal." In fact, besides my mother, I was the only person I routinely lied to. I lied to my mother out of habit, even if there wasn't a reason to do so. Telling the truth didn't score me any points with her, so I learned to lie if it was easier to do so. I lied to myself to avoid having to unravel the complicated judgments she'd made about me. For example, I convinced myself that my mother hated me because I was an awful person. That was easier than sorting out what role she played in our dynamic—and it also gave me more control.

On the contrary, I still believed my dad was a great father. All dads were emotionally absent, withdrawn, and distant, right?

I knew my grandfather scared the hell out of me, but I had no clue why.

Maybe that subconscious tie to another broken person was the bond between Dawn and me, though. She was raised alone by her mother, because her abusive father was in jail. Maybe it was because her pain complemented mine, but I felt a certain comfort around her. We didn't have books in common, we didn't have science in common, but she was smart, she was kind but fiercely tough, and she was perfectly broken when I needed someone like that to let me know I wasn't alone. I wasn't weird or out of place when I was with her. I was where I belonged for the first time ever. So I couldn't have cared less what my parents thought of her.

We identified very well with each other. She was a fantastic friend. She stayed with me through what were arguably some of my angriest years. This seems to have been the starting period during which my subconscious first began trying to chew on and process *so* many painful, buried memories. But it's hard to say for sure, since I was so angry for so long. I don't think many people could have tolerated me through this period, but she did. She helped keep me grounded and hold things together.

I graduated magna cum laude from SUNY Oswego with a double major in physics and math in 1995. I moved to Columbus, Ohio, to attend the Ohio State University's nuclear engineering graduate program. I moved there with Dawn. That was the beginning of the end of our relationship. It was her first time away from home, and she fell into a pretty party-oriented crowd. I was more business-minded than ever as I looked to get ahead and find new ways to be successful. Our diverging paths led to a parting of ways about one year later.

I met the woman who would become my wife a few months later. I met Jill in the late summer of 1996 shortly after Dawn and I broke up. Jill had just finished graduate school and was working toward her certification as a speech language pathologist. Having just finished school, she was still living with her parents in the Columbus, Ohio, area.

I was still a couple years away from completing my graduate studies. I knew I had to work a summer practicum in Los Alamos, New Mexico, in the coming summer, so I wasn't sure if I should get out and date anyone yet. I figured it didn't hurt to at least test the waters and see who was out there. I was not a "bar scene" kind of guy by any measure. My life revolved around school—and up to that point, my girlfriend—so I really didn't know anyone in town who I could meet women through. As such, I joined a dating service.

I met a few women. We had nice dates, but nothing that rocked my world. Then Jill saw my profile and asked me on a date! I thought she was breathtaking from the first photo I saw of her. Her profile came across as the sweet, affectionate person I really wanted to start growing forward with. I accepted.

We were like a couple of old friends hanging out for the first time in years, the minute we met. We went to Highbanks Park on the northern end of Columbus and walked the paths for hours. We followed up with dinner and then watched the movie *Tin Cup*. We had such a wonderful evening, she invited me back to her parents' house so I could meet them. On the first date! Time with her felt so natural and comfortable, it didn't even intimidate me to go with her. I figured someone as wonderful as this must have great parents.

I may have been falling in love with Jill within moments after meeting. Nobody else I ever knew touched my heart quite like she did. She was beautiful. Still is. Her hair. Her face. Ahem, her body. All perfect. She was dressed professionally yet comfortably for our date walking the trails at Highbanks Park. She was well educated, and very smart. She was so sweet—and so very thoughtful.

Jill's parents were equally amazing. They were well put together. They were welcoming, happy to invite me in. They were engaging. They asked a lot of very thoughtful questions. Their house was beautiful—furnished and decorated in a sophisticated yet inviting way. Jill had finished graduate school and was living with them while she finished getting her certification in speech-language pathology. They loved and respected each other enough that this arrangement did not place undue stress on any of them. Jill had a life I would have given anything for growing up. I was in awe of her—and adored everything about her.

Her parents welcomed me into the family with open arms. It's really a joke that today, we still carry the baggage of this name we—Jill, me, and our kids—share. We don't have anything to do with that God-awful family. We truly are part of Jill's family—not the family whose name we hold. It's been a joy over the years to belong to a true family.

Jill and I got married in 1998. About five years later (2003), we found out she was pregnant with our oldest daughter, Addie. Very soon after that, we found out my mother had terminal pancreatic cancer. My father had accepted an early retirement deal from Kodak, and they were living in Florida at that time. Jill and I flew down to spend a few days with them before my mother died.

While there, my father unloaded a lot of information on me about how abusive my mother had been to me. Almost immediately, some repressed memories began coming back into focus. I had convinced myself she hated me, because I was an awful kid. I had learned to handle that concept, because in that scenario, I was in control. If I hadn't grown my hair long through high school and college, if I hadn't blared Slayer on my stereo so many times, if I hadn't worn Megadeth T-shirts, then I could have been a "good kid" and she would have loved me just like she loved Bryan—in my mind. It turns out, though, she hated me just because I was so undeserving of love. There's nothing I can or ever could have done differently. She hated me just because I was so deeply and fundamentally flawed that I was unworthy of love—under any circumstances. At least that was my immediate take on it.

The house of cards I had built to pretend I controlled my mother's feelings about me was collapsing. As card houses do, it was collapsing quickly.

I had built that house, because I *needed* to believe she hated me for a reason. A reason other than because I was not worthy of love—not even of my own mother's love. Being forced to face the apparent reality of *how unlovable I was* threw me into a tailspin that lasted for years and led to new, even more disturbing revelations—which added years more to the tailspin.

CHAPTER

6

Interactions with
My Father as an Adult

TO BE FAIR AND HONEST, I sometimes find it difficult to pass judgement on someone who has endured the hardships my father faced. He was the oldest of seven siblings. When I was a freshman in college in 1992, he came to me to tell me some things about his father that should have shocked and disgusted me. His revelations did neither.

My grandfather had recently died, and this caused a cascade of abuse memories at my grandfather's hand to come back to many people, including one of my cousins—according to my father. My father's recount of what an evil man my grandfather truly had been only panicked me. I had no idea at the time why these accounts panicked me. I really didn't even give my reaction any thought at the time. Today, I think it's because my subconscious had been fighting a fierce battle to keep a lot of information locked down, and with this revelation, it knew it was about to lose the war.

My father told me his father had physically, emotionally, and sexually abused him and all of his siblings. He claimed he wanted to make sure he hadn't attacked me in any way, as he had supposedly attacked one of my cousins.

Apparently, my grandfather's death prompted one of my cousins to reveal that she'd had an interaction with my grandfather one night while sleeping at our grandparents' house. The abuse, as my father put it in 1992, is reportedly why my cousin had absolutely refused to set foot in my grandparents' house beyond the age of about eight. My father told me her revelation had started a chain reaction through the family, unearthing years of buried memories of abuse. My father and some of his siblings apparently never forgot the terror.

That was what my father told me, anyway. But the story changed over time. Initially, he said his dad had abused her. Years later when I began questioning my father about specific details associated with his father, he recanted that statement and told me he didn't know and had never heard anything about such a "story." The details of what my dad would say about my grandfather—and even the label he put on him—were inconsistent over time.

Despite retaining memories of his father's abuse, or possibly because of this, my father insisted that my family spend every Saturday at his parents' house. It's beyond my comprehension how a person could live through such abuse and still dedicate one day every week to spending time with his tormentor. The only possible explanation I can think of is that he condoned and perhaps even agreed with that type of behavior. It appeared that my father visited my grandfather frequently because he thought my grandfather was a real stand-up guy who had some great ideas about what it took to raise a child properly.

Even more perplexing as I unraveled these pieces was, how could he allow his own two children to spend two unsupervised weeks with the man who so abused and tormented him and his siblings? The answer to that question seemed clear to me, and the same as before. My father thought, despite his momentary lapses of admitting otherwise, that my grandfather's abusive ways were the only proper way to raise a child.

The incident when I was five in our kitchen with the milk carton and my mother rushing to Bryan's and my aid was normal behavior to my father. It showed the true rage that burned within him when my brother and I were very young. The incident perhaps shed some light onto the person he really was—and would remain. My mother hadn't put herself between my father, my brother, and me just because it was a convenient place to stand. She saw something in the way he was posturing and looking at us. His rage wasn't just that of blowing off steam. It was building and boiling over into something much more, something much worse. How, then, did she tame him so quickly and effectively?

When Jill and I visited my mother and father while my mother was dying in 2003, my dad took me aside to frequently mention how horribly she treated me, as I've mentioned. He reminded me all about her put-downs and constant picking at everything I did.

"You know, I always tried to defend you," he added. *A bald-faced lie.* He was too afraid of her to stand up to her.

But there was another element he described, which I believe may be based on fact. He said there was only so much he could do, because she had threatened to use every legal angle she could to take us away from him if he got in her way. As I mentioned, that may be why he never left her, even when he had an affair. I'm guessing how it really went down in the situation with the milk jug was that she threatened him to the utmost extent of criminal punishment if he ever physically threatened any of us again, as it seems he had that day when I was five. My mother's strength and extremely dominant personality, which often manifested itself as abusive toward me, in this situation actually balanced my father's apparent desire to physically abuse Bryan and me by completely and thoroughly dominating him. Perhaps on that day, we were in the eye of their storm, with a temporary reprieve as their abusive natures swirled around us.

The storm that was my parents stayed alive, however. When my brother and I were in high school, Bryan had a girlfriend who lived in a troubled home. Her dad and older brother routinely beat and harassed her. One day, she called Bryan. She was locked in her bathroom with her brother and dad pounding on the door, trying to get to her to beat her. Bryan sought advice from my mother, who in turn asked my dad what they should do.

My father very angrily responded, "She should just take her beating— sometimes *all kids just need to take a beating.*"

My father's exclamation was such a spontaneous, gut-level response, it was hard to imagine there wasn't at least some part of him that truly believed that. The evidence seemed too hard to ignore. He enjoyed spending much of his free time with a pedophile who had raped and beaten him routinely, he put Bryan and me in harm's way by leaving us alone with this psychopath for weeks at a time, and he openly admitted he felt children should be periodically beaten. My dad clearly stood by his father, because he was so warped by his upbringing that he couldn't even see how evil my grandfather was.

To the contrary, my father's actions and words seemed to condone the evil my grandfather represented. By my dad's view, my mother had "robbed" him of his "right" to raise us properly. "Properly" in his mind would have been, of course, delivering periodic beatings, or worse. Since my mother would have killed him—possibly literally—if he laid a hand on us, he seemed to have found a work-around for it. He knew if we stayed at his father's place, it was just a matter of time before our grandfather would give one or both of us the beating that we "deserved."

I grew to understand how he developed this work-around through years of counseling and probably cumulative years of very deep soul searching and meditation on the facts that I had available. Each memory I unearthed led me closer to this final conclusion, that my own father purposefully sent my brother and me out to my grandfather to be beaten and possibly raped by the man he had no doubt at all was an extremely violent and dangerous pedophile.

I came to believe there's a special place in hell for people like my "father." I put father in quotes, because real fathers would go through hell and back to *protect* their children.

As I sought to make sense of life with my parents—and grandfather— my father came somewhat clean to me in a series of emails between us in the late 2000s. He admitted that he had actually helped my grandfather "abuse" my aunts and uncles. My father may have been alluding to tormenting his siblings with physical beatings; however, when Bryan and I were young, we tended to snoop through my father's drawers looking for "reading material." We would typically find *Penthouse* or the occasional *Hustler*, but sometimes we would find short pornographic storybooks with the saying *The Family That Plays Together Stays Together* scrolled across it. They were small enough to hide—usually less than five inches tall and a quarter of an inch thick. In it were twenty or so short stories of families in incestuous relationships. Occasionally, these stories even involved teenage boys molesting their preteen sisters.

Based on my father's words, his actions with Bryan and me, and his choice in literature, I came to believe that he did not look back on the events of his youth as torment at all. Rather, I believe he longed for the days when he, too, could wantonly molest little girls and physically torment smaller, weaker children.

Even today as I write this book, my father's primary motivation is to abuse those around him. Both Bryan and I have extended a helping hand when my father was in need. We've both extended an olive branch to him every time he's said extremely hurtful things to us while in the midst of mending fences from his last attack. Most recently, I reached out to my father several years ago and had what I thought was a good conversation. Within weeks, he wrote a long email to my brother about all the things he hates about nearly everyone—and included me only to say, "And there's Kevin. I could write a book about him." He'll never get the opportunity to add any chapters to that "book." I decided that I'm done letting him hurt me.

My last correspondence with my father came in early January 2018. He messaged me out of the blue on Facebook. It was the first time I had heard from him in years. It was a very confused, poorly-written tirade about all the evils he felt I had done to him and my mother over the years. My response follows:

Ron,

This is in response to your message sent via Facebook Messenger on December 15, 2017 (copied below for reference):

[My father's original message is in the first "paragraph," my response follows below the dashed line. I copied his tirade in my response to him so he could have an opportunity to think about how convoluted and disorganized his tirades tend to be.]

I have to say I'm sorry. I've kinda shut you out of my life and gave no reason to you. You have never treated me with any respect. At your wedding, you told us to wait outside and you'd have somebody come and get us to have the pix taken. We were not picked up, After Mom passed, nothing changed. At my wedding you ignored Marilyn [my father's new wife] and I. You came to Florida, and it took weeks to get to spend some time with your family. It got so that when I came into a room you and Addie [my oldest daughter] would go somewhere and play. At Addie's birthday party, you shunned us and when Addie refused to acknowledge us you laughed it off. I think that the only time you've ever called was when you lost your job near fathers day and you called from Columbus. I never knew whether you were calling for financial help,advice or to wish me happy Father day.

I don't really care. You can't show me any
respect and I can't live like that. I love
you, as I always have. I'm not mad, I just
can't deal with being treated like you
were treating me. It used to hurt badly to
not be a part of the grand children life,
but they picked up from you that I don't
deserve to be respected. If you should
ever want to contact us, our new number is
*** ***-****.

I disagree with most of the events /
"facts" that you list. I'll specifically
address some of them in this letter. There
is one fact, however, that I am in perfect
agreement with. You are absolutely correct
in saying I don't respect you.

For several years, I have had a growing
number of unresolved questions building.
I tried to address one of them with you
many years ago—regarding memories that were
still very fuzzy at the time—but you chose
to sidestep the question. The memories have
come into much better focus, and now I have
many more, but different questions.
I always try to keep an open mind, but
from my understanding/knowledge of past
situations, it's difficult for me to come
to conclusions different from where I
currently stand.

The following sections break down some
items. First, I cover a few specific points
from your note above [the "paragraph" above
the dashed line]. After that, I cover my
understanding of the past through memories

*I've recovered and talks I have had with you
and other family members. These provide the
background required to understand why I have
to acknowledge that I don't respect you.
Those sections bring me to a final conclusion
that very clearly lays out the direction I
need to go for my own health and for the
good of my family.*

A Few Points From Your Note
What My Children Have Picked up From Me
*You were not only right about my absence
of respect for you, you are also right in
saying my children have picked up traits
from me. I'm not sure how you would know
this since you haven't seen them since
Addie was about two or three, but THANK YOU
for acknowledging this! You are completely
correct. They are extremely empathetic and
loving. They are hardworking. They're smart
and outgoing. They love playing games or
volleyball as a family. They're extremely
funny. They're beautiful. They're confident
but not conceited. Above all, they know
they are loved. That was something I never
had until Jill managed to work it into my
head how much she and her family love me.
It was my second self-imposed directive
for my children (the first being to protect
them from harm at all costs)—to make sure no
matter how hard life gets for them, because
it WILL have its moments, they always know,
beyond ANY doubt at all, that their parents
loved them through and through. Nobody will
ever be able to take that away from them.
I never had that, but they'll never live
without it.*

Financial Help

Yes, I was laid off once. However, that happened between November 2011 and March 2012, years after we moved to Tampa, at a time when Jill's business was killing it and we could have lived indefinitely off her income. If I called you and told you I was laid off, it was one of the many calls of its nature where I tried to just say, "Hi, I'm here; Let's talk; What's up?" and open a line of communication. NEVER since Mom died have you called US like that. You emailed a few times for the first few years after she died, but never called. Additionally, if we were going to seek out money from a family member at a time like that, it would have been from Jill's parents. They've been more fortunate through life and have more than enough money to help their kids out. They've given a couple of Jill's siblings large loans (even when they know they will never pay them back). I'm sure the KODAK pension wouldn't possibly allow for that, even before it was taken away. Since we know them far better, borrowing from them would make more sense, anyway. Fortunately, it never came down to that during that period.

Last time I called you (just to once again extend the olive branch, despite the horrible and mean lies you write about Bryan and me—and I tried to say "hi"), KODAK had just canceled your pension program. While I never even considered asking you for money—even when I was laid off—you definitely seemed to be fishing for hand-outs in that call. You didn't come out and ask, but it was clear enough you were

looking. The pathetic thing is that I would
have helped if I could have. I actually
considered for a moment taking out a loan
to do what I could to help you out, despite
how vile you've treated Bryan and me. After
all, you're (biologically speaking) my
dad. We were in the middle of a very rough
transition/reorganization at the family
company, and it was sucking every resource
we had and then some, so there was nothing
I could do. We were already slipping into
debt at that point ourselves.

Wedding Photos
You also reference something about photos
at our wedding. Since that was almost
20 years ago, and this is the first we're
hearing about it, I don't think it's
possible to track down exactly what
happened there, if anything. Jill has
wedding photos the photographer took with
you and mom in them—suggesting you were
not left out of the photo shoots. As such,
I'm not sure what the miscommunication was
since you were in the official pictures. It
may be that it was a very hectic day, as
weddings are, and something perhaps misfired
in the coordination.

Lack of Contact/Uncaring "Grandfather"
When Mom was on her deathbed and Jill and
I came to Florida to visit with her, you
spilled your guts to me about a lot of
things. One of the things you confided was
that you regretted having children, and
you didn't really want anything more to do
with us. You also admitted how keeping in
touch with family was just too stressful,

because it brought up bad memories of Mom. You said a lot of derogatory things about her, particularly about the way she always harassed me (I believe your words were that she would "nit and pick at everything you did"—referring to me). You even relayed a story of how Mom, to that day, still would dig at me. She apparently went on and on about what a failure I was when I delayed defending my master's thesis a few weeks to stay in school for one more quarter (while earning tuition and a good stipend). In your 12/15 note and in the numerous other times you've sent these types of letters/ notes to Bryan and me since her death, you seem to like portraying yourself and Mom as victims. You've even gone as far as to talk about how great Mom was to me in some of your correspondences.

Again, you try to portray me here as the one putting up walls. No, I'm not calling every holiday or birthday, but I have reached out on many occasions despite the laundry list of reasons I have to not do so. You, on the other hand, have made good on your promise to cut Bryan and me out by NEVER calling. Not even a card or phone call for your grandchildren who you moan so loudly about in your note above, yet you make ZERO effort to be part of their lives.

Mom's Role in Our Lives

Your statement that Mom would "nit and pick at everything you did" while she was dying agreed well with everything I've remembered and discovered. It seemed as if she was always mad at something. More often

than not, that something was me. When I
was very young, I tried my best to appease
her. I tried everything to earn her love. I
pretended to like things or dislike things
just to try to have something more in
common with her. The expectation I had with
that was, if I was more like her, perhaps
she would like me. It didn't work. That
only succeeded in hurting me more. Not only
did she apparently dislike me for me, but
I was trying as hard as I could, and she
still seemed to hate me. By time I reached
middle school, I changed tactics. If I
couldn't win her affection, then I would
earn her hatred.

What made me feel that my own mother hated
me? In day-to-day life, she typically tore
me down at every opportunity. The "nit
and pick at everything" I did attitude.
Growing up, it seemed hateful, demeaning,
and that she genuinely didn't believe in me
or want me around. Even my relatives from
New England noticed her poor treatment, if
you'll recall. After visiting with Mom's
parents, Uncle Raymond and Aunt Sandy, and
Aunt Gail one summer [I believe it was the
summer between 4th and 5th grades], they all
got together after we left to discuss how
they could help me. They were concerned
about the way she was treating me. They
were afraid it could have very damaging
effects. A therapist I once saw said this
was a classic intervention, and pointed
out that people only get a group like this
together and come to a singular consensus
to intervene in someone's personal life
when there's a unanimous and often times

urgent concern that the person is behaving
in a way that's dangerous to themselves or
someone else. This wasn't something done
on a whim, in other words (as Aunt Gail
can also attest to). They left it up to my
grandmother to call Mom and try to reason
with her. My grandmother and Mom had a very
strong relationship, they reasoned, and
talked frequently. One would expect, then,
that my grandmother would be able to at
least plant a seed. She called and spoke
with Mom. It was nearly a year before Mom
would even talk to her again. Even then, I
heard the relationship was quite tense for
some time after that.

My Aunt Gail went on to help as much as
she could without risking being completely
blocked out of Mom's life. She pushed to
get Mom to let her have me for as much time
every summer as possible. According to
Aunt Gail, her goal was to expose me to a
situation in which I could feel I belonged
and was appreciated for as much time as
possible each year, even if that was only
for two weeks.

Mom also frequently told people what a
disappointment it was to have had a second
boy instead of a girl. Again, when you and
I were talking when Mom was dying, you
feigned ignorance in rhetorically making
the statement, "I don't know why you and
your mother never got along better." When I
responded that it was because I was a boy,
you looked at me almost fearfully. "How
did you know that?!" you asked. I told you

*it was obvious. I knew before I ever began
kindergarten.*

*I have a vivid memory from when I was in
kindergarten about one of my mother's
blatant put-downs regarding how disappointed
she was that I was me. Mom took me out to
lunch with her cousins after I had school
in the morning. We finished lunch, and
they got me a small sundae with sprinkles
on it. Her cousins were joking about the
sprinkles being "fly turds" and that I should
give them the sundae to take care of it.
Somehow Mom worked into the conversation
what a disappointment I was since I had the
audacity to be a boy. Her cousins looked
at me aghast, likely expecting me to break
down in tears upon hearing how much my own
mother hated me. By that time, however, I
was already so accustomed to her hatred that
I cracked a joke about how yummy the "fly
turds" were to try to lighten the mood to
make them feel better.*

*I could give many more examples of her
yelling at me when I'd get hurt or sick, or
just her general put-downs. For instance, I
once sliced the side of my leg open (about
a 3-inch long, deep gash) with a broken
piece of glass in a bag we were taking to
recycling. I had blood running down my leg
and soaking into my sock. Both my hands
were covered in blood, because I was in a
lot of pain and trying to stop the bleeding
by holding the wound. She literally yelled
at me to quit being such a baby, clean it
up, and keep helping. It ultimately took
nine or ten stitches to sew the wound*

together enough to make the bleeding stop.
By the way, this was the summer between
fourth and fifth grade. Jill still wonders
to this day why I hate when she tries to
help me when I get hurt or when I'm sick.
A couple years ago I had a bad case of the
flu with bronchitis and pneumonia starting to
set in, and I almost jumped down her throat
when she offered to take me to the doctor.
I'm just very well accustomed to taking care
of myself and don't like the emotional abuse
that would always go along with accepting
help for any problems associated with wounds
or illnesses.

All my life, I felt that Mom hated me. This
feeling has changed a lot with a couple
memories I've recovered over the past
five or so years. Years ago when she was
still alive, her apparent hatred caused me
nothing but pain, so yes, I avoided contact
most of the time while she was alive. If
it hadn't been for Jill's demands that I
stay in touch, I would have parted ways
with both of you decades ago. When I feel
Jill's being too hard on the kids, I step
in and diffuse the situation as she does
with me. You were well aware that mom hated
me because I was a boy and could see it in
how she treated me, and yet did little to
nothing to diffuse the tension between the
two of us. This is one more reason I don't
respect you.

Summer Trips to Your Father's
When I was a freshman in college, you
took a very commendable step and brought
up a very difficult topic. We were alone

*together in the car one night when you
brought this up. Your father had recently
died, and [my cousin] had come forward to
say that something had happened to her
while staying alone at their home when she
was little. You told me about her "run-
in" with your father. You also told me
about all your siblings, with the possible
exception of Patty, having been routinely
molested and beaten by him. You admitted
at that time that you and some of your
other siblings were well aware that he
was a child predator even when you had us
spend unsupervised time with him. With that
knowledge, you had Bryan and me spending
weeks at a time alone with him, for several
summers of my childhood.*

*You asked me during that conversation if
he had ever molested me while Bryan and
I were staying there. I very defensively
and quickly (I may have started answering
before you even finished the question)
shot back a "NO." I had little memory of
anything in my childhood at the time, and
honestly had no memory of run-ins with your
dad, but it immediately concerned me why
I wasn't at all surprised to find out your
father was a serial child molester. That
kind of news should be enough to stun the
most emotionally numb person.*

*Over the next 20 or so years, I have slowly
pieced together a considerable library of
childhood memories. I've even advanced
to the point where I can remind Bryan of
things that happened. Unfortunately, along*

with the good memories unlocked, I've also unlocked some horrifying memories.

I won't get into the details of what I've recovered. It's unlikely much of anybody would believe me, even if I said what had happened. Let's just say my "no" response was a bit over-optimistic.

So, what does this have to do with respect? Many things:

My self-imposed, number one role with my children is to keep them safe at all costs. Conversely, you sent Bryan and me to stay with a man you admittedly knew was a sexual predator for two unsupervised weeks each summer. The second summer I even protested. I didn't want to go, but was basically forced to.

When I came home with my face extremely swollen (one eye swelled tightly shut), I have absolutely NO doubt you knew exactly why it was swollen. You may not know the exact scenario that transpired when your father beat me until I was unconscious, but you had to have known he did it. Even Mom knew something was up. She couldn't stop examining my face—looking for clues as to what really happened, then quizzing you on your thoughts of what could have happened. She desperately wanted to help me, but I didn't feel I could let her—reason number one, she's one of my heroes now—she was determined to help me, but I didn't trust her enough to allow her to do it. Her questions were followed by your insistent protests of, "It's poison ivy!" I couldn't

*tell the truth for several reasons, and
just wanted Mom to go away and stop looking
at me.*

*You were a scientist! It didn't take much of
a scientist to figure out that if a kid's face
was exposed to enough poison ivy in smoke to
swell it the way mine was swollen, he should
also have died from respiratory distress.
Instead of coming forward and asking me some
tough questions, you led the charge on the
lie that it was caused by poison ivy.*

*Bryan asked me once why you never asked him
about being molested. I'm certain this is
why. I believe that you knew your father
did that to me, so you singled me out in
the questioning and didn't bother asking
Bryan anything.*

*When I called years ago because I was
just starting to get some memories that
seemed to be getting a bit cohesive, and
I was looking for some help to pull them
together, you LIED to me and told me your
father was virtually a saint. You claimed
Uncle Les was the sicko who would attack
children. "Why do you think your cousin
John is gay?" you pointed out.*

*That call seemed to be a significant turning
point. It wasn't long after that you
began writing derogatory things about me
to Bryan. My takeaway on this is that my
questions and knowledge make you nervous.
That's why you lied to me—trying to throw
me off the track. Then belittle me to
others to discredit anything I may come
forward with. The more I know, the more*

*you're aware I can pull all these pieces
together. Pieces that point straight at you.*

*Your behavior since Mom died has been
extremely destructive. You've sent numerous
hate emails and messages to both Bryan
and me that don't seem to have any cause
or intent other than to hurt. Your need
to hurt others (especially Bryan and me)
has evolved from putting Bryan and me into
harm's way at your father's hands into
cyber-attacks. Without Mom there to keep
you in line, they've been perplexingly
belligerent and unprovoked.*

*There's more that ties into all of this.
When Bryan and I were very young—even he
was too young to have any idea how old
he was—we each remembered an incident
as clear as day. You got home from the
grocery store and were off the rails angry
at us. Mom felt compelled to step in to
set up a human shield between you and us,
suggesting she felt you were going to come
at us physically. Reason number two she's
one of my heroes now. She sent us to our
rooms, so I have no idea what she did, but
I don't recall ever seeing you nearly that
out of control again. Whatever it was that
she said or did, she clearly took control
of the situation and household in general,
and never relinquished that control. She
wasn't going to ever put up with that type
of behavior. Fast forward to when Bryan and
I were in high school. Bryan's girlfriend
at the time lived with an abusive father
and brother. She called Bryan in a panic
one day, and when the question of what to*

do got to you, you angrily replied that
she needed to take her beating because kids
"need to take beatings sometimes".

What do those above bullet points tell me?
It tells me you had abusive tendencies that
led you toward thinking violence against
Bryan and me was an acceptable, and probably
even desirable, alternative. Mom asserted
her dominance early on and would have had
your head if you laid a hand on either
of us. To get around this, you kept your
upbringing a secret, so Mom would have no
idea what kind of person your father really
was. That left you open to send Bryan and me
out to your father for a "proper" handling
as soon as we were old enough for Mom's
comfort level in sending us out.

I've been working extraordinarily hard
to fight through a lot of very painful
memories. I can finally sleep through most
nights without nightmares now, since I've
reconciled most of the memories. I'm still
missing one of the most difficult memories,
because quite frankly, what I've seen of
it scares me too much to let it all the
way out. However, I've assembled a very
comprehensive recollection of very difficult
moments. These moments could not have
happened if Bryan and I had parents that
gave a damn about us. Ultimately, the root
cause of those moments leads to you.

The only reason I can think of a parent
allowing one of their children to stay with
a known sexual predator is because they are
angry. They're angry that they were hurt,
and their spite has driven them so far that

they're actually willing to take out that hurt and anger on their own defenseless child.

CONCLUSION

I'm confused by your extremely erratic and unpredictable behavior: you tell me YOU don't want anything to do with Bryan or me; you live up to that promise by never instigating any type of contact except these extremely venomous notes for nearly a decade; then you accuse ME of shutting YOU out. YOU fish for financial handouts after your pension is taken away, then accuse ME of coming to you for money. I'm hopeful that even you can see the significant and fatal flaws in your positions here?

You took a backseat as Mom ran all over me while I was growing up. You acknowledged that you were fully aware that she hated me because I was a boy, yet you did little or nothing to get between her and me. You also stepped aside, or even worse, DELIVERED Bryan and me to your father into what became for me a living nightmare.

Your lies and cowardice do not deserve respect.

You seem to be living in your own reality. Beyond that, you are extremely destructive—you have been for as long as I can remember. You purposefully seek out the meanest things you can come up with just to cause pain. You purposefully tried to hurt Bryan and me as children, now you're still trying to inflict damage in a new way.

I'm done. Do not call me, email me, or contact me in any other way. EVER.

A portion of his response to my January 2018 letter follows. I've been asked by some why I wouldn't just delete it after giving him an ultimatum to never contact me again. In short, I hate him more than most people will likely hate another human being, but he *is* still my father. I was hoping he would actually acknowledge my pain. Perhaps an apology would be too much to expect, but an acknowledgement. I read his response, because I was hoping against hope for something I could actually hold onto. I wanted to give him the benefit of the doubt and see if he could possibly tell the truth and actually work on rebuilding some type of relationship. I give you what I received to work with:

> Dad was an alcoholic, but functional and with good self-control usually. He could drink beer or mixed drinks and be as normal as anyone else and was "civilized," exercised judgement and self-control. But when he got plastered, he became uncivilized and had no or little control. I don't believe that either you or Bryan ever saw that side of him. If I thought that he was doing that, I'd have severed the contact.
>
> During the early 50s we met Steve Dickerman. He owned the farm across from Uncle Dave, where the church is now/next to Amico's. Steve brewed "HARD" cider down in his root cellar. Dad liked it and put in two barrels of cider the next fall and worked it. He liked the results, but Dave lived across the street and at the time was a bad alcoholic. Dad was born in '18, Dave '20, and Paul '23, and all 3 were alcoholics. The four older brothers and Peg, the baby ('30) were normal.

Dad would drink the "HARD" cider by the
water glass. After three or four glasses
he would start to change. After a couple
of quarts, we would leave and stay away
if we could. Anything could get a violent
response. Dad continued to brew two barrels
a year until the late 60s when he stopped
the cider. But he brought the cider from
Penfield to our house in Rochester and he
would drain those two barrels himself. I
don't know if a barrel is 50 or 55 gallons.
While home on leave in '66 I tried to
drink some. Could not do. Burned all the
way down, and within twenty minutes had
diarrhea, and that with just a swallow.
TERRIBLE stuff, and he was drinking 100
gallons a year.

When he went off, his right hand and arm
became a club, and he would club you high
to knock you down. Then he would kick,
kick, kick you. If you tried to get up,
the left hand would take you by the hair
and hold you about thigh high, and the
right hand would grab something on your
back (belt, shirt, whatever) and slam you
into whatever was around, wall, car, frig,
stove, tree, whatever.

When he was fifteen, he challenged his dad
and nearly got killed. He crawled to the
neighbor farm (Judd Brown) and got his
health back and worked for his keep at
Judd's. He swore that he'd kill any of us
just as his dad almost did to him. He was
living his training, sorta.

One summer, as referenced in my 2018 letter to my father, I returned from my grandparents' house with one eye completely swollen shut and the rest of my face slightly swollen as well. It was so bad that my mother took me to the doctor to have it investigated. I made it clear in this letter to my father this was not slight blistering from poison ivy. He went on in his response to my letter to stand by his original lie, reiterating his claim that I simply had some blistering on my face from poison ivy, no swelling of any kind. Nothing out of the ordinary. He continued to praise himself for what a wonderful job he'd done in raising my brother and me. Granted, we didn't grow up in the environment he had, but I give *all* the credit for any safety we had in our home to my mother. She was far from reaching sainthood, but she stood up for me when it mattered most.

I was stunned by his response. I had laid my soul bare, and he simply danced around most of my particularly difficult talking points and blatantly lied about others. The statements my father made in these 2018 emails dismissing his father's abuse contradicted many of the things he'd told me up until that point. His letter took me back to my freshman year in college and the talk he and I had. During our talk, my father had pointed out that conditions were so bad in his house growing up that one of my aunts purposefully got pregnant when she was a teenager, so she would have to move out with her boyfriend/new husband. He told me that the physical and sexual abuse were extremely pervasive in the house. These statements were reinforced with an email he sent me on January 25, 2008. His denial of my grandfather's true nature in his 2018 response prompted me to dig up that old email, which stated:

```
I grew up in a family that was full of
sexual and physical abuse. No belts or
spoons, but kicked and slapped around.
I grew up being abusive to my siblings,
it's what I learned in Family 101.
```

He appeared to be sugarcoating the truth in 2018, after being called out as an abuser himself. His more open and honest statement in 2008, when he did not feel backed against the wall and defensive, paints a somewhat different picture from his 2018 statement. He describes a scenario so saturated with violence that, as the oldest, he even perpetrated the same crimes against his own siblings.

My therapist (Dr. Watson) and I saw this in him years earlier when he attended one of my sessions to "help" me get a grasp on the past, and instead he vilified me for an hour. Dr. Watson and I spent many sessions afterward puzzling over what had happened. She concluded that a lot of victims of abuse put their children in harm's way in an effort to control a situation where they felt helpless as a child. Later in life when they realize they hurt their child by doing that, they create an alternate reality for themselves. Often, it's one in which they were the hero instead of the ultimate villain they truly were.

I have difficulty seeing my father as anything other than a complete liar. He was *not* a victim if he was victimizing his own siblings through childhood, as he admitted to doing.

His reference to spoons and belts points toward disciplinary methods that had been employed in our house as a matter of routine while growing up. My mother's weapon of choice to beat Bryan and/or me was a large wooden spoon. I recall relatively routinely getting whipped by my father with a belt, particularly when we were out at his father's place. My brother doesn't remember that, but he doesn't seem to remember much of anything that ever happened at my grandparents' place, good or bad. His memory of things that happened at our house seems almost photographic, so it's peculiar how little he remembers about trips to our grandparents' house. He only remembers being whipped with a belt when my father visited one of his old, abusive navy buddies. Whether to fit in and follow suit with the discipline his friend was dolling out on his kids—or because the irresistible temptation to beat a defenseless kid presented itself—is debatable. My father's reference to belts in his 2008 email suggests accuracy in my memory of it being more routine than that one time.

The more I read his 2018 statement, though, the more I see a thinly veiled confession. He closed his argument by saying his father threatened to kill him and any of his siblings if they dared to challenge him.

I didn't bring something very important to my father's attention about this—something I had spent years struggling to sharpen into focus. I knew he would call me a liar. I could handle being called a liar about a great many things, but not this. I once knew a little boy who was only seven years old during the summer of 1980. The boy refused to look away while his evil grandfather mercilessly did something dreadful right in front of him. The defenseless boy refused to stand aside and allow it to happen. He nearly paid for it with his life.

I think my father saw that helplessness in what I had written. I think he really did remember. I think somewhere inside, he still knows the truth, which is why he included that statement. He was letting me know he was aware that I was witness to my grandfather "living his training."

7

The Blonde-Haired Girl

SOMETIME AROUND 2011 OR 2012, my memories of the summer of 1980 with my grandfather began returning with a vengeance. The therapist who helped me digest the memories as they came said repressed memories don't typically begin to resurface until something either forces them to come back—such as someone talking about their experience with that person—or until you're at a point where your subconscious mind feels you can handle the extreme stress.

The first memory came very quickly, seemingly out of nowhere. I was overcome with extreme sadness while driving home. I was getting a vision of my grandparents' family room. It was such a powerful memory I had to pull off into a parking lot. I was in their family room, sitting in my grandfather's chair, looking out a window that overlooked the driveway and most of the front yard. At first, I was looking primarily at the empty driveway, hoping that by some miracle Grandma and Bryan would return home. I knew, though, that my grandmother would be gone until almost sundown. By the look of the shadows, it was nearly high noon, so I had hours to wait until they returned.

I thought hard about what I needed to do. I needed to tell somebody about what had happened. In this memory, I didn't know exactly what had happened, just that it was truly awful. As I stared out over the "cigar tree" and front yard, I first thought of telling my mother. I crossed her off the list, because she was more likely to blame me than help me. *I could tell my father*, I thought. His typical response to anything was to say "hmm" and refer the question to my mother, so I decided he wouldn't be of any help. Then I thought of my brother, but I knew his go-to move would be to tell Mom and Dad. This would lead to me getting in even more trouble, because my mom would accuse me of trying to get away with whatever she would accuse me of having done.

I realized for the first time that I had no one. There wasn't anybody on this planet I could rely on or go to, not even in a crisis of this magnitude.

As I considered my predicament, my attention was drawn to the flies swarming around the outside of the window. I was mesmerized by them. When one wanted to leave, it just flew away, off to a better place. It could find new friends and a new place to live there, or it could just exist completely alone.

I longed so much to be that free. I longed to get out of my life. To get away from my current situation. To get away from a mother who hated me. To get away from a father who didn't really care one way or another about me. *Just to get away.* To start over somewhere else.

I had to get away. I obviously needed the food and shelter provided by my parents, so I had to find another way of escaping. I realized I could emotionally detach myself from the situation, effectively removing myself from where I was, while still physically being there.

Based on what my father told me about my grandfather after he died, and based on the extreme power of the sadness and fear in the family room memory where I contemplated how alone I was and was mesmerized by the flies, I assumed he had molested me in some way prior to that memory. As far as I know, to my forty-eighth year on this planet, I was wrong. It was worse. *A lot worse.*

The next memories came to me in bits and pieces out of chronological order.

I know I can't adequately convey what happened during that day in the summer of 1980. I'm not that talented. Nobody is. I'll just lay it out on the table for you to see. Expose it to the light. Perhaps you won't understand. You probably won't even believe it. But for me, perhaps shining light on it will scare some of the demons away—and burn away some of the hurt.

Help Me!

My grandfather was leading me into their bedroom. Along the wall to the left in the bedroom was a miniature half-door that led to a small storage room. One of my grandparents' nightstands was usually in front of the door; but this time, the nightstand was pulled out sideways away from the wall. The miniature door was open far enough for me to see inside.

Inside, I saw a girl, probably about Bryan's age (ten or eleven, maybe just a little older). She was as far to the right-hand side of the room as she could get without hitting her head on the sloped ceiling. She was sitting on the floor on her bottom, with her feet flat on the floor in front of her and her knees up near her chest. Her heels were tightly pulled up into her thighs and bottom. Her arms were tightly wrapped around her knees. She had straight, blonde hair that was down to about the middle of her neck. She was skinny with a hard, tomboyish face and body.

Grandpa had me go into the storage room with her. I sat down right beside her, next to her right shoulder.

I whispered extremely quietly to her as I got near, "It's OK. He's my grandfather."

Having said that, I sat ever so slightly behind her right shoulder, perhaps hoping this older girl could help protect me from whatever this was. I didn't want her to be so scared though, so I hoped to make both her and myself feel better with my statement.

The next thing I remember is him forcibly removing her from the storage room. I only have one snapshot of this in my head, but it's a brutally painful image. He has her by the left arm. She's turned somewhat facing me, her left arm getting pulled kind of behind her, her right hand reaching toward me. We either were holding hands in the room and had been pried apart, or we were reaching for each other as she was getting dragged out of the room.

I don't think this next memory will ever fade. It's one of the only memories that still brings tears to my eyes at the slightest thought of it. He was attacking her in some way. I've assumed he was raping her, but I don't know. I don't remember leaving the little storage room. I don't know if he forced me to, or if it was somehow less scary to be in the bedroom than in the storage room. For whatever reason though, I was in the bedroom facing the wall between the bedroom and the bathroom. I was desperately trying to block out what was going on behind me. I couldn't, though.

She was screaming. Not a scream like a couple kids on a playground. Not a scream like an actress pretending to be scared. Not a scream someone lets out when another person jumps out from around a corner. I've heard my young girls scream in a lot of pain when they've hurt themselves roughhousing. Even that doesn't come close. I have nothing to compare this scream to. The only way I can describe the scream is to say I listen to the scream in my head nearly every day. It has been running over and over for at least a couple years now. This scream is horrifying enough and troubling enough that despite my exposure to it, I have tears dripping down my cheeks as I write this, once again reliving it. There needs to be a word more powerful than scream to describe this. Terror, pain, hopelessness, loneliness. Each feeling and emotion stronger than the next, all rolled into one horrifying sound.

She was screaming, then cried out, "HELP ME!"

I thought, *what a great idea! Now an adult will come help her*! My head jerked up toward the door to watch someone come put a stop to this. That person never came. *Oh, yeah*, I thought to myself. *We're all alone.*

She started screaming again and cried out "HELP ME!" a second time, and I realized she was calling out to ME.

I was kind of mad. *Why is she calling out to me?? I CAN'T help her! He'll just kill me too!* I argued with myself. I reasoned that if I stayed out of sight in the shadows along the wall, maybe he wouldn't hurt me like he was hurting her. I couldn't help her. I was just a little kid! I immediately felt ashamed of my decision and excruciatingly guilty.

Then she cried out a third time, "HELP ME!"

That was the end of my debate. I didn't care at that point. I knew helping could be a literal death sentence, but I also knew I couldn't live with myself if I didn't help. I had to try. I *had* to do *something*. I ran over to the foot of the bed. They were lying long-ways across the bed. I put my hand on his forearm and in a whiney, seven-year-old voice, said "Stop!... You're hurting her!... She's my friend!"

That seemed to open the full fury of hell. I looked over to her face for a second and have a very brief shot of her looking at me with shock and relief. Her expression said everything. She never, in a million years, expected me to actually help, but she was beyond grateful that I had.

In that instant, time stood still. Neither of us knew or cared about the hell that was about to be unleashed.

My attention was quickly redirected back to my grandfather. By this time, he had risen up onto his knees on the bed. I could feel the rage coming off him. It's odd. In my memories, my grandfather is nothing but a silhouette. Just a black, human shaped void. I'm guessing that's my subconscious at work protecting me from the most horrific element of the attack. My grandfather's hatred and anger were palpable in every way.

The next thing I remember is feeling like I was in one of the room's corners somewhere. I couldn't see, and I felt like I was getting heavily tossed around. It was also extremely loud. The sound was like a jet engine–some type of loud fan or white noise. I felt like I was in some strong river rapids, struggling extremely hard against getting tossed into rocks. The roar of the water was deafening me.

I was very quickly losing strength. I was constantly moving my arms. I don't know if I was throwing punches or trying to block punches. I also don't remember any pain, but I suspect he was hitting me, and that was causing the sensations of getting tossed around.

In addition to tossing me around a lot, the intensity of such a fight could have spiked my blood pressure. The white noise I heard could have been the sound of blood rushing inside my head and ears. I could have been losing strength from trying to defend myself or throw punches. I also could have been losing strength, if I were suffering repeated blows to the head and/or body.

I remember thinking at one point: *So this is what it feels like to die. It's not as bad as I would have thought.*

Eventually I became convinced I had already saved her, so I could let go and die. I'm not sure why I thought I had succeeded.

For whatever reason, I went ahead and let go. That was a decision I hated myself for even before I had recovered this memory. To this day, I don't know if I had actually saved her, or if I had failed her and left her to die alone.

I've spent years trying to determine why I was so certain I had saved her. I've desperately attempted to recover a memory of her fleeing, or some other tangible piece to hold onto.

Recently, I was reading through accounts of near-death experiences. I have always found those to be fascinating. Often hard to believe, but fascinating nonetheless. This was the first time I heard this type of account, though. A person reported having an "out-of-body experience" after suffering a heart attack on a pier. He flew past his two children. When he saw them, he briefly stopped and thought he couldn't go on, because they needed him. The way he reported the assurance washing over him that his children would be fine without him, and that he felt absolutely sure it was alright to let go, stunned me.

I never saw God or any long-dead relatives ushering me to "the light." I never left my body and saw other parts of the room. But I did feel that strange and absolute self-assurance that *she would be alright*, and a sense that I needed to *just let go*.

Also, there wasn't just a lack of pain in the experience; there was almost a true serenity, only hindered by my conviction to save the blonde-haired girl. In the midst of taking this beating, I was going through the motions of fighting only to save the girl. I personally felt so peaceful, I was hardly even aware that I was fighting.

Could that strange assurance that she was going to be fine have come from something other than one of my known senses? I was committed to fighting to the end for the blonde-haired girl. I stopped only because I knew she would be safe. The entire experience was odd enough that I can't, with confidence, rule out anything—no matter how seemingly far-fetched.

I obviously didn't die. Why not? I was ready to. I almost wanted to. If she was going to die, then so was I. It felt so peaceful in the midst of the chaos.

As I uncovered this memory, it left me with a very big, almost insurmountable question: *why am I still here?* And other thoughts soon followed: *I'm wasting an incredible gift—at a second chance to life. I'm going through the day to day, just like everyone else. I'm still here. I should be doing so much more with this gift. I've overcome so much–I'm supposed to make a difference.*

8

Unraveling the Pieces

I CONTACTED MY COUSIN IN THE SUMMER OF 2020. This was the same cousin who my dad had initially told me in 1992 was abused by my grandfather. I could barely bring myself to reach out to her given how intensely painful another rejection of my feelings would be. She was only about three years older than me, but I hadn't seen her since I was a very young child. My memory of her was that she was too adult-like, too far beyond my level of maturity, for me to be worthy of bugging her. Somehow the child in me could still show his insecurities well into adulthood. Additionally, my father basically had called me an outright liar to say anything had happened to me at my grandparents' house. My brother's inability to process it or deal with it made me think he looked at me as a liar, too. I was not sure how I could possibly absorb another family member's rejection.

I was desperate, though. I needed answers. There were many loose ends I needed to tie up. My father was lying to me at some point. Either he lied that my cousin was abused, or he was lying later in life saying he had never heard of such a "story."

Also, I *needed* someone in my corner. It's devastatingly lonely fighting a battle of this magnitude without a single person who really knows the truth on your side. You know the truth. You vividly remember the scenes, but everyone that matters calls you a liar. *This, theoretically, was an easy one*, I said to myself. *Am I alone in witnessing his abusiveness and in having the willingness and strength to address it, or did my cousin truly have some type of traumatic run-in with my grandfather?*

Her response amazed me. She hadn't had any altercations with my grandfather of that nature. My grandfather did throw her across the kitchen into a set of cabinets once when she was very little—perhaps about five—because she was standing in his way. But he never sexually attacked her in any way.

She was, however, very reassuring, sympathetic, and welcoming. She was abundantly familiar with the family history and knew my experiences were at least credible. We ended up talking on the phone for quite some time. We caught up with each other, we shared some traumatic and some fun family memories, and we talked a lot about nothing in particular. Talking with her, I finally understood what it was supposed to feel like to have family of your own.

In talking with her, I found the answer to one question, but I opened up a much larger one: *why did my father make up that story about my cousin's abuse?* Not only did he lie about my cousin coming out about her abuse by my grandfather, but he wrapped it into an entire story about the account spreading through the family, causing a massive upheaval and explaining why we never saw our cousin after we were little kids.

I wrestled with this question for some time, but ultimately came to the suspicion that my father needed a segue to ask me if I remembered being abused while at his parents' house. He could have simply used the topic of his father's death as a segue, though.

Such a convoluted lie seems a bit extreme for that explanation, I thought.

I realized that my father had gone to great lengths to isolate me that night and ask this of me without my brother around. The more I thought about that, the more certain I became that he knew something had happened when I came home from his father's house with my eye swollen shut and the rest of my face very swollen.

In a conversation I had with Bryan, my brother angrily asked me, "Do you know why Dad never talked with *me* about Grandpa's true nature?" He was quite upset that our father wouldn't feel free to confide that to him as he apparently had to me—and to make sure he had been unharmed through the years. I thought long and hard about why my father may have ignored Bryan in such an enormous matter.

I finally came to an undeniable conclusion that connected all the dots. One day I shouted to myself, *my father never saw any signs of abuse in Bryan!* Beyond that, my father had such a strong relationship with my pedophile grandfather that the two of them almost certainly discussed the details of who my grandfather abused and how. My father never asked Bryan any of those questions, because he didn't need to. I realized that I could all but guarantee my father knew exactly what abuses occurred to me while I was at my grandparents' house any time I stayed there.

My thoughts continued exploring the evidence, and I concluded that my father was doing nothing more than testing the waters to see if I *remembered* any of the abuse. He used the lie about my cousin as a segue, because it allowed him to feign how harmless he thought my grandfather was up until he supposedly learned about my cousin's abuse.

I came to believe my father had simply concocted that story to pretend he was looking out for me, even though he was actually working against me—trying to set me up to be abused by his father. Based on his lie about my cousin, I believed in 1992 that my father had only just found out that my grandfather was still actively pursuing children well into old age. My father came to me to "make sure I was alright," so the story went. But he actually was attempting to establish his lack of fault in any of it. Concocting such a convoluted lie in 1992 was basically an admission of guilt in knowingly sending my brother and me to that pedophile for a *proper* upbringing when we were young children. My father built that story around that particular cousin, having no idea that at some point down the line, social media would tie everyone together, allowing me to reach out to her as I did. If it weren't for modern technology, I never could have found her, let alone spoken with her to learn about my father's lie.

Throughout 2019 and 2020, I searched a lot of information in my head and tried to "connect the dots" in an impossibly convoluted puzzle. *Why did my father reveal the true nature of our family to me in 1992 and throughout more than a decade through smaller discussions, only to start fabricating a different reality later?*

Pre 2009, my father describes his family life as being very violent when he was a child. His descriptions of my grandfather were very frightening.

When I approached him around this time because I needed help with some difficult memories that were just beginning to resurface, he agreed to attend a therapy session to help me, feigning interest in my well-being. Instead of helping me to heal, he defended himself. He told Dr. Watson all about what a "horrible kid" I always was, how much I "always lied," and that I was nothing but "a lot of trouble."

I puzzled over why he frequently sent out hateful messages about me or to me after 2009, like the one in the 2018 letter. I tried to piece together why my father's response to my long list of facts in the 2018 letter didn't even attempt to address any of the substance, except for his continued claim that my face was swollen from poison ivy.

I came to some cold, hard conclusions.

First, he couldn't even begin to defend himself from the facts in my email, and he had to have known it. This is why he deflected the conversation into a long soliloquy about the distant past and side-stepped nearly every point. He did a complete about-face and described a very *civilized*, downright friendly father, who would on occasion threaten to kill his children.

A "civilized" father threatening to kill his children?! It was an extremely desperate and ineffective attempt to re-write history. Everything he's ever told me since 1992, in fact, paints the same portrait—that of a very violent upbringing where everything was fair game, up to and including death threats and an obvious willingness to follow through with those threats.

The second thing I realized in my soul searching was that my father is very well aware that, at the very least, my grandfather beat me nearly to death because I challenged him in some way. He may or may not know what I challenged him on, but he would not have included the paragraph about my grandfather threatening to kill any of his children who dared challenge him, unless he knew I had experienced that level of hate from him for that exact reason.

It became clear to me that my father purposefully delivered his own children to a pedophile so they would be abused—or in his mind, appropriately treated. *What kind of sick, twisted creature does something like that?* He has feared the day I put the pieces all together. That's why he would frequently verbally attack me, both to my face and to others, and lie about how horrible I was to Dr. Watson—for an hour. He was desperate to hide the past for very good reason.

When one works with a pedophile to deliver kids to them, that by extension makes the delivery person a pedophile, too, right?! A *very* good reason for him to want to re-write history.

9

Seeing the Grey in My Parents

MY PSYCHIATRIST HAS VERY ASTUTELY POINTED OUT that everyone is a shade of grey. Some are closer to pure white. Others, like my grandfather, are painfully close to pure black. She has been quick to point out that I need to see and acknowledge the grey in my father, not just the black.

I can see where she's coming from. I have a lot of good traits from him. He was often playful—initiating a quick game of "gotcha last" where we'd basically tag each other and try to get away quickly. He also took time to play board games or card games with my brother and me as we grew up. He taught me the value of a hard day's work—doing yard work or other chores with him. He also taught me the value of hard work just by the example of having finished night school to earn his bachelor's degree while working full time and raising both Bryan and me. That last one was all in the name of building a better life for all of us. My psychiatrist pointed out that he likely married an extremely strong woman in my mother to help ensure that he did not carry on the family way of beating and abusing Bryan and me; he at least made a strong commitment to attempt reversing the evil.

My psychiatrist has further pointed out that nearly every victim of abuse ultimately sends their own kids into harm's way at the hands of their abuser. She claims it's not a spiteful, vindictive, or even conscious move. According to her, the parent is still looking for control over the situation. Subconsciously, they think that, as an adult, they finally have control. They feel they have such ultimate control at that point that they can even send their own kids into harm's way, and it will work out.

I interpreted that to mean she was absolving people like my father of their crime. As such, I had a few words for her.

She quickly pointed out that recognizing the reasoning for an event, and hopefully ultimately forgiving the event and person who caused it, does not necessarily mean that one does not see the event or person as wrong or evil. She said there are reasons it happened that I need to recognize, but the act was absolutely still wrong.

In far too many cases, these thought patterns in survivors of abuse do not work out well for their children.

For numerous reasons covered, it's clear to me that my father was very well aware I had at least been physically abused by his father. He could have ended it there, in 1980, when he saw the swelling in my face. Instead, he continued forcing us to spend unsupervised time with his father for years to come, against my protests. He lied to me, my therapist, and Bryan at a minimum, trying to discredit me and throw me off the track of recovering my memories. The weight of the evidence reinforced to me that he helped orchestrate the abuse with my grandfather. He was not innocent in this. He purposefully sent his children to a predator to be molested. For that, I'll never see him as anything other than the same evil piece of crap his father was.

THE APOLOGY

I had a notable exchange with my mother in 2003 that I would be remiss to not mention. Jill and I were sitting with her in her living room in Florida when she was dying. This was one of my last conversations with my mother, maybe even the last one. I wish I remembered her words more clearly, but at the time, it was just a lot of additional garbage being spewed by her that didn't matter to me. She apologized. She apologized for "everything;" for *the way she had treated me.*

She was looking at me expectantly, presumably waiting for me to break down in tears and exclaim that I forgave her and all was well. I did my best to force out some tears. That would have been a true Academy Award moment though, if I could have mustered up even a single tear for a woman I hated so deeply at the time. I was sure she was only apologizing because she was afraid she was too evil for heaven and destined to go burn in hell for all of eternity.

My father could hear the apology from the kitchen. That later set him off on a tirade about what an *empty, meaningless bunch of crap* that apology was. He went on to say something like, "She can't just undo a lifetime of suffering with an 'I'm sorry!'" That led into him going on about her abusive nature and some of the evils she had done to me through the years.

For years, I agreed with my father—and my initial instinct about her true motivation for the apology. For whatever reason, that apology came up in a conversation with my psychiatrist sometime in 2019. She told me I needed to grab that apology with both hands and hold it as a prized possession. Apparently, very few parents ever apologize for abusive or inappropriate behavior. She went on to say that parents do not give out apologies unless they are very much aware of the transgression they have made. Further, awareness alone isn't enough. She almost certainly had to truly regret the actions to make such a statement. In other words, it should not be taken as a fake statement.

I have the two memories of her protecting me—or doing her best to protect me—and a deathbed apology as a bargain against all the other horrible moments. At this point, I can only conclude that she really did love me. I don't know what stressors she grew up with. I do know her mother was someone none of the grandchildren looked forward to being around. My grandmother was rather short tempered and surly. I always blamed this grumpiness on her significant arthritis problems, but perhaps that had always been her personality. Perhaps she was very hard on my mother, and my mother, in turn, saw that as an acceptable way to treat a child. Perhaps that's why my mother was so desperate to have a girl. She wanted a girl to spoil, so she could undo her childhood pain and traumas, much as I shamelessly spoiled Addie for the first couple years of her life.

My mother's disappointment in not being able to undo the pain likely led her to treat me the way she did—something she realized close to the end of her life. Did that mean she *didn't love me*? I don't think so. You can look at these three very significant moments in my life alone and conclude there wasn't anything she wouldn't have done for me, including stepping in front of a raging bull to stop his charge. These moments are what make her my hero today.

My therapist has concluded it's very possible that the moment Mom put herself between my father and me when I was very little was likely more of a defining moment in my life than any of the traumas. She said the empathy I've always exhibited had to come from somewhere. Empathy is most likely learned from someone close to us. She feels that my mother more-or-less throwing herself on a grenade for me when I was very young and still very impressionable could explain why I tend to look out for others and do my best to avoid hurting anyone unless they hurt me first. I've decided that *I almost certainly learned that from my mother.*

When I first started this book early in 2020, I started writing about my mother first. As you've read, there are portions of this book that have nearly nothing nice to say about her. Those were some of the first passages I wrote. The healing process is a wonderful thing. Moving past the hurt sometimes allows you to see the good in people that has been obscured by the pain. My mother went to great lengths to protect me when things really mattered. She acknowledged her pain at how she treated me at times outside those moments. She truly did love me. To me, that means *everything*. I don't know what demons she was wrestling with that prevented that from showing through more often, but my mom loved me. I can't write that often enough. I'm sorry I've only been able to realize that now that she's been gone for seventeen years.

10

A Vision of Black

BEFORE ANY OF THE MEMORIES of the blonde-haired girl arose, I had a vision of a black-haired girl. All of my other memories brought extremely clear pictures of the surroundings, the people, and the emotions. This memory, however, didn't have any background. It was just all black. I don't know where I was. The emotions were almost crippling.

Over the course of about three or four weeks as the memory came into better focus and I processed the pain from it, I would often have to leave work to go for a walk and get my bearings, because I would start sobbing uncontrollably.

When the memory first started coming in, I knew it had something to do with my grandfather, and I knew it was extremely painful, so I automatically assumed it was a memory of him abusing me. Then I got a flash of a young black-haired girl. She was maybe six or seven years old. I didn't have a clue how she fit into everything, but the fact that this beautiful, sweet, little girl was somehow involved in this nearly killed me. I felt I could handle any memories involving just my grandfather and me. In that case, I'd know that I'd survived, moved on, and thrived.

A memory involving someone else, however, left the questions: *Where are they now? Did they survive? Were they able to pick up the wreckage and put it back together?*

The girl was on display with her arms folded across her stomach. She was wearing a beautiful, white, lacy dress with pale blue flowers, each with four petals ringing the upper part of her arms and chest. Her hair was about shoulder-length, wavy on top, and curly on the sides and back. I couldn't make out details of her face, but in general I could see she had very soft, smooth features.

I'm devastatingly sad in the memory. I've just seen her for the first time, and I'm torn to pieces by the sight.

At the same time, I'm terrified. I know my grandfather is nearby. I'm afraid to show any emotion. I need to convince him that I'm not bothered at all by what he's done. If I show any pain, he'll know I'm on her side, and he'll almost certainly kill me too.

Following years of picking apart this memory and the others, one of my therapists concluded that the black background and black hair on the girl represent death. The extreme emotional load in the memory is likely because this girl was the sum of all the pain associated with the blonde-haired girl, along with the possible visual representation of her presumed death. It's the releasing of all that cumulative pain. It came out first, before the image of the blonde-haired girl, to prepare me for the actual memories. Further, she surmised that the girl herself may have been a representation of the innocent child that died in me. It's perhaps represented as a girl, because it's easier to view that way, given that my grandfather likely molested me on another occasion based on recurring nightmares I used to suffer. The female representation of oneself apparently helps make sense of such a twisted assault.

This interpretation is a bit muddied by something that my grandfather did late in 1987, though. When I was in ninth grade, my grandfather hired a company to bring a backhoe out to his property to dig a hole the exact dimensions of a grave.

The only exception on the dimensions is that this "grave" was about six inches shallower than a standard grave. Given how evil my grandfather always was, it's very disquieting to me that he dug what he referred to as "his grave" on his property, and for years I couldn't fully reconcile exactly what this memory, real or fabricated, of the black-haired girl really was about. I also still don't know what he ended up using "his grave" for.

Furthermore, the grave was located on the property in a place where he could easily look out the window next to his Lay-Z-Boy chair in the evening and see it at the end of his day. His property was largely clear, and the hole could have been located in any number of places given the size of the yard. Was this purposefully a location that allowed him to admire his prized possession at the end of each day? It seemed too small to be useful for disposal of much yard waste. He claimed it was to dispose of some rocks; however, the rocks that he claimed would go in the hole were on the other side of the yard, a good 100 or 200 yards away. Why dig the hole so far from the materials to be disposed of? Also, wouldn't it cost about the same to have the rocks hauled away as it would to pay someone to bring a backhoe out to dig a hole?

He had it dug late in the autumn. He was going to fill it in the spring, but ended up filling it a good month earlier. What opportunity presented itself weeks earlier than anticipated? *What is in that hole?* I asked myself.

Along those same lines, my grandfather almost never left the property. I'm only aware of him leaving the property once. That one time occurred when a black cat they owned got its leg cut off on my grandfather's table saw. Supposedly, the cat jumped up on the table while my grandfather was sawing some wood. The cat somehow then got its leg cut off by the blade. I've often wondered how a cat gets a clean cut perpendicular to its leg by a saw blade that most likely was at least nearly straight up and down. One can very easily see how a psychopath would get angry that a cat jumped into his workspace, grab the cat, and forcibly cut its leg off. In any case, he ended up leaving the property to rush the cat to an emergency vet.

A psychologist I saw for several years puzzled over why my grandfather may not have left the property for years at a time. When I told her about "his grave," the lightbulb went on. She speculated there were secrets he needed to ensure nobody was seeing on the property. What those secrets were may never be discovered, but she felt a lot of questions fell into place—between his apparent cruelty to animals and people, unwillingness to leave the property, and the digging and subsequent filling of "his grave."

I never talked to my grandfather at all, and he never really attempted to interact with me, except on the day we drove out there and I saw "his grave" was filled in. I typically kept a wide berth around him. I had no memory of any bad events with him when I was younger, but I knew he was a terrifying individual, and even as a young child, I would have nothing to do with him. "Why did you fill the hole already?" I asked him point blank, almost challenging his decision to do so.

He shot me his usual scowl, mumbled something incoherent, and walked away. I don't remember what was going through my head at that time, but for me to not only say something to him, but to downright challenge something he did suggests I had a strong feeling he had done something terrible. I was challenging him on that action, just as I had when he was attacking the eleven-year-old blonde girl.

Another recurring nightmare, seemingly unrelated to the two girls, which I experienced for a long time involved being grabbed from behind by a very tall, skinny, strong entity. My brother and I were young children in this nightmare. We ran across a cobblestone bridge in what looked like an old Italian village. We split up. We each desperately tried to open a few doors on select buildings, but before we could try very many of them, I was overtaken by this entity. It grabbed me from behind. I wildly threw punches over my shoulder, trying to get the entity off me, but none of my punches were effective. The nightmare luckily ends quickly after that.

Dreams can represent a wide variety of truth in a person's thoughts or memories, but it doesn't seem to take very deep thought to interpret what my subconscious might have been trying to tell me in these nightmares, especially when considering what kind of sick freak my grandfather was. Compared to me when I was a child, he was tall. He was always very skinny. And he was an evil looking creature if there ever was one.

CHAPTER

11

Search for the Girls

I RESEARCHED AND FOUND that the New York State Police have jurisdiction over the portion of Livingston County where my grandparents once lived. They have missing persons and homicide reports listed on their website dating back well into the 1970s. There isn't anything matching either the blonde-haired or black-haired girl—or any young girls that went missing during any summers, for that matter.

That could suggest the black-haired girl truly was a conglomeration put together by my subconscious in an attempt to help me digest all the horrible memories I was about to get hit with. It lends evidence to the blonde-haired girl escaping the ordeal alive as well.

I was convinced the blonde-haired girl had been killed. Even before I had any conscious memory of the events, when my girls were very young, I adamantly taught them that if anyone threatening approached them, they needed to get away by whatever means necessary. I taught them to grab and twist in certain areas if they could, or kick or punch those same areas if possible, and especially taught them over and over how to bury their fingers to the knuckles in the attacker's eyes and wiggle their fingers around in there. When questioned why they should be so gross and brutal, I assured them a fate worse than death awaited them if they didn't beat their attacker, so *nothing* was off limits or too gross. I believed in that teaching with every ounce of my soul even years before having a conscious visual of my grandfather's attack.

I believe I was so convinced that the blonde-haired girl had died, because my grandfather likely told me he had killed her. I must have had my grandfather reeling. He fully expected me to turn the other cheek compliantly and obediently as he brutalized that poor little girl. He knew how to read the situation. He knew my father was such a weak, sorry excuse of a man that I couldn't turn to him. He could easily see how much my mother and I hated each other. Without any support, I was his for the taking, so he thought.

When I rose up and ruined his plans, he had to go into damage control. He cleaned up the scene and somehow sent the girl away. He couldn't kill her, because if he couldn't silence me, then he'd have to answer to murdering a child. I'm not sure what he could have possibly told her to keep her quiet, but I'm sure someone as experienced with brutalizing children as he was could come up with threats and actions that would work.

Then when I woke up, somewhat concussed, he could tell me that he'd killed her, and that I'd be next if I breathed a word to anyone.

In my memory of the black-haired girl, I choked back my emotions, because I was afraid if my grandfather saw me cry over her, he'd think he couldn't trust me and would kill me too. I had to choke back my emotions, because my grandfather was right there telling me the blonde-haired girl was dead, and I had to be alright with it to live.

This was the year I ended up going home early, because I "was exposed to poison ivy in the smoke of a bonfire." As referenced, the "poison ivy" swelled one of my eyes completely shut and caused swelling over other portions of my face.

This is what my mother wouldn't stop examining. Her mother's intuition was strong. She knew damn well poison ivy didn't do this.

I still can't believe nobody asked the question, "How did his face get so severely covered in poison ivy, yet he didn't inhale any of it and end up in the hospital—or dead?!?" My mother even took me to the doctor to get a real answer.

The doctor was a spineless bitch, though. She basically took a look at my face, took a step back, and asked "Kevin, was this poison ivy?" That tells me she knew it wasn't but didn't want the liability of calling someone a child beater.

BITCH! I was terrified. I think I took about half an hour to answer the question. *Would the doctor call me out as a liar if I went along with the poison ivy story? Would I then be in even more trouble for the blonde girl's death? If I came clean, what would happen to me then?* I took a chance and said, "Yes, it was just poison ivy." I think the doctor knew better but didn't want to get in the middle of any child abuse drama. *Spineless BITCH.*

Armed with the belief that the blonde-haired girl may have lived, I approached a private investigator in 2019. I gave him a brief synopsis of what had happened and why I was seeking her. He declined to take the case, saying he really needed an address or name to work from to find someone from so long ago. He did give me some tips to find her, however. Using his pointers along with some of my own ingenuity, I may have found her.

It turns out there was a young girl who would have been eleven years old during the summer of 1980 living a short 1.25-mile bike ride away from my grandparents' house. I first verified she lived there through means available to amateur investigators online. My personal verification showed she lived there at least by 1986, but I couldn't find information dating back to 1980. I later had a private investigator named Chris Holland in the Rochester area confirm she lived there at least as far back as 1980.

Keep in mind, this was a very rural area. There were probably only five houses within that distance of my grandparents' home in 1980.

In addition to that, I found a picture of this woman in 2019 in a local publication. She was hidden behind a mask for Halloween, but a girl I believe was her young daughter was there (she shared the same last name, according to the caption). Her daughter had perfectly straight, blonde hair, just as I remembered the blonde-haired girl having in 1980. I sent a short message to a couple of email addresses reportedly linked to her, but I never received a response.

I initially assumed the emails were no longer valid, so in 2020, I revamped my search. I found her Facebook profile. Her profile picture was exactly what I would have expected to see from my memory of her when she was eleven. Seeing the profile picture took my breath away for a couple seconds, because it was so similar to my memory of the eleven-year-old. Now up around fifty-one, her profile picture showed an adult version of the eleven-year-old etched into my memory. The profile picture showed a skinny blonde with straight hair. She was dressed in simple clothes—a T-shirt and shorts. Every bit consistent with the skinny eleven-year-old with straight, blonde hair who looked to be at least somewhat of a tomboy.

The system allowed me to send her a note via Messenger. I wrote a scaled-back version of the email I sent in 2019, which follows:

Hi [first name],

I'm sorry to send you this bizarre email. I have been haunted by an event from my childhood (summer of 1980) and am hopeful that you may be able to help me lay it to rest. My name is Kevin Vought. I was born and raised with my older brother in Penfield. My grandparents (father's parents) lived on Lake Road in Avon (Richard and Leora Vought).

The Cliff's Notes version is that my grandfather was quite possibly literally a psychopath. He routinely beat and raped all seven of his kids, one of my cousins, and likely many more. My father made my brother and me spend a couple weeks alone at their house each summer. I think 1980 was my first summer there. I was seven at the time. I'm almost positive it was that year that he abducted a skinny, blonde girl, most likely 11, but perhaps as old as 13. She had straight, blonde hair cut about midway down her neck. She seemed tall, but that may be because she was a few years older than me. I vividly remember his attack on her, and getting beaten to what felt like near death when I told him to stop hurting my friend.

When I woke up, neither he nor the girl were anywhere in the house. I've been told by everyone under the sun that I was only seven and didn't stand a chance against a grown man, and if he killed her, it wasn't my fault. Just let it go. If I hear that from one more lame ass person whose most difficult childhood memory is having to settle with the smaller Barney doll, I'm going to lose it! I COULD have fought him harder. I could have forced that piece of crap to kill me too, then she wouldn't have died alone.

I felt certain while fighting him that I had saved her, but I don't have any idea why I was so sure of that. Perhaps I saw her run away? I'm hopeful I'm right and she did

*live. I talked to a private investigator
in Rochester to chase her down and another
little girl I remember from years later
(1988). He bowed out saying records were
too sketchy from that far back and that
there was pretty much no way to find those
girls. However, I am almost positive my
brother and I played with the blonde haired
girl, which is why I probably referred to
her as my friend and was so comfortable
with her when I first saw her in the room
(before it became really obvious to me
how much danger we were in). As such, she
probably lived close-by-so it seems she
shouldn't be too hard to find.*

*Thanks to the power of big-brother and
Google's ability to search the databases, I
see you lived on Lake Road in frighteningly
close proximity to my grandparents in
1986, and that you're right around the
age I remember of the girl. If, by some
weird stroke of chance, you were the girl,
then I can't tell you how sorry I am about
dredging up such a horrible memory. Rather
than time making this easier, it seems
time is only increasing my guilt and the
pain of that day, and I more and more
overwhelmingly NEED to find out if I managed
to save her from that lunatic.*

*If you're not that girl, did you know
anyone in that vicinity that fit that
description at the time? If so, was she OK
after the summer of 1980?*

*All I want to know is-was she relatively OK
after that day?*

> *Thank you for bearing with me through such*
> *a ridiculous email-and thank you even more*
> *if there's any info you can provide on this*
> *mysterious girl in my memories.*
>
> *I don't sleep much, so please feel free to*
> *call me any time on my cell at 813-[completed*
> *phone number] if you have anything to share*
> *and prefer to do it that way.*
>
> *Thank you SO much!*
>
> *—Kevin Vought*

The private investigator who confirmed her address through 1980 also confirmed both of the emails where I tried to reach her should still be valid. I made every effort I could think of to reassure her and prove that I was a real person. I wanted her to know for certain I was not some type of identity theft bot in California just trying to scam her. I made sure to specify Lake Road, because I found it hard to believe any bot would ever be smart enough to steal the remote street in an off-the-map town like Avon, where someone lived prior to 1990.

She had my profile in Facebook to look at, in addition to my wife's profile and our company's profile linked from my wife's site. Even with all that and what I felt was an extremely heartfelt plea for help, I did not get a response. Facebook verified the message was sent. I never received any error messages from the sent emails. As far as I could tell, she received all three messages.

Weeks after I sent the Facebook message, I tried to friend her, thinking that maybe her settings would block messages from unknown people, even though Facebook reported that it was sent. She has over five hundred friends, suggesting she is relatively open to accepting friend requests from most people whose profiles do not appear too suspect.

Her lack of response to any of my attempts to communicate could come from at least a few sources. She may not have been the blonde-haired girl (now woman) and thought I was trying to scam her. I attempted to make my message clear that I was simply looking for help in finding someone. Further, I left my Facebook settings wide open so she could see I attended high school near Rochester, I earned my bachelor's degree at SUNY Oswego nearby, and I had several friends from both my high school and Oswego linked to my account—which should help verify I went to both of those places. Additionally, what scammer would go to such lengths to pretend to have a connection to the road you lived on thirty to forty years ago? I just couldn't believe someone with over five hundred friends on Facebook would be paranoid enough to be that fearful of people.

Many people reading a message like that may question the sender's mental health. Again, I populated my Facebook account with my current job, educational background, and a number of pictures of my wife and kids to help show I was just an ordinary, family-oriented guy. In my Facebook message to her, I even gave her Jill's full Facebook name, so she could look there as well. My very detailed profile could be found on LinkedIn, and a simple Google search would bring up other facts at least from my work history. Those wouldn't necessarily prove I was sane, but it is likely exceedingly difficult to be the CFO of a successful small business and maintain a great marriage and home life if you're not exactly firing on all cylinders. Given the nature of the plea in the two email messages and then the Facebook message, I would like to think at least most people would put a couple minutes into digging out whether or not the sender is legit.

Many people will throw out a message after reading the first line and deciding it must be spam. Perhaps that's what happened to the emails. That doesn't necessarily explain the friend request being cast aside by someone with an established openness to accepting friends. Also, I don't believe spam messages are much of a problem on Facebook. If a person gets flagged for spamming too much, their account can apparently be shut down. As such, a knee-jerk reaction to just deleting a message in that format doesn't make as much sense as in email. Given the openness of my profile, the general nature of Facebook messaging, and my ability to corroborate who I am and what I do with my wife's well established Facebook page, I didn't think a knee-jerk assumption of spam was at play here.

The one unifying explanation that could tie everything together is that she remembered, at least in part, the attack. She was "the blonde-haired girl." I was so traumatized by the attack that I buried the memory almost instantly, kept it hidden from myself for about thirty years, then only managed to resurrect and process the memory through a great deal of emotional effort with abundant help from trained professionals. All that trauma and effort, and I didn't even experience half the trauma she went through.

I was an observer. I *heard* the screams.

She was the one so terrified, hurt, and lonely as to let out screams of that nature.

I was aware of some kind of attack.

She was being *brutally* attacked, while I stood there arguing with myself whether I should help or hide.

If the tables were reversed, I would likely be doing everything in my power to push anything that even came close to reminding me of that day completely out of my life, too.

When I first saw her Facebook profile picture, I lost my breath for a couple seconds. I was absolutely looking at the adult face of the little eleven-year-old etched into my memory. To me, her almost frightening resemblance to the eleven-year-old I remember, her proximity to my grandparents in 1980, and her adamant resistance to acknowledging my heartfelt attempts at communication all but definitively verified she was my grandfather's victim.

It's a shame I couldn't seem to break through to her if she was the right person. I completely understand her need to keep it all away.

But I have so much I still would like to say to her.

Perhaps with this book, I can. I'd like her to know she's my hero. She was brutally beaten and likely raped by a man for whom the moniker "evil" doesn't do justice.

Beyond that, I have to believe she left that house that day thinking she had witnessed my grandfather beating me to death. She, like me for many years, probably thought she was responsible for my death, as I blamed myself for hers. Despite those horrendously deep scars that no kid should ever have to bear, she picked herself up and made a good life for herself.

Perhaps she blames herself for portions of my grandfather's attack that were aimed at me, similar to how I blamed myself for her death. She may never have even read the complete messages for fear of what they would say, what accusations they may throw at her.

I hope that's not what she thinks, because my feelings for her couldn't be further from that. I just want her to know how very happy I am for her, knowing that she's well, and that she's my hero.

12

Evolution of the Vision of Black

As I wrote this book, I searched through parts of my memory I honestly had left far behind years ago. There were a handful of thoughts and memories I had perseverated on at the expense of some of the others. I focused on the particularly traumatic memories and all but forgot about the seemingly more mundane ones.

The danger in doing that is that all the memories fit together to tell a complete story. When properly aligned, even the seemingly mundane memories can begin to take on a more sinister undertone, or at least help explain exactly what was happening in the traumatic fragments of memory. Each fragment by itself is nothing but a sliver of the whole reality.

When I recalled numerous fragments, some of them seemed like they began fitting together to move the story of the black-haired girl along.

When I was in eighth grade, something happened between Bryan and me that ended up being one of the very few memories I had from childhood that I actually never forgot. It always struck me as an extraordinarily odd memory to retain, given how many other seemingly more dramatic memories had been so well buried.

We were at my grandparents' house in Avon on one of our Saturday day trips with the entire family. We had just walked outside to throw the football around. It was cold, with a couple inches of snow on the ground. It was either very overcast or getting a bit late in the evening, as it was relatively dark. We walked out on the driveway with my brother holding the football. I was about to go running into the large yard, but I noticed him staring very intently at the house somewhat across the street. I say *somewhat* across the street, because there was nothing but a farm field directly across the street and pretty much as far as the eye could see to the right. To the left, however, was a fairly narrow, two-story house.

The family that lived there was outside. It looked like they were getting ready to go somewhere. It deeply irritated me that Bryan was staring at them. I asked him in an annoyed voice why he wouldn't look away.

He said it was because they had a little girl. I glanced over at their front yard and could see that they did indeed have a little girl who was about five or six years old with black hair.

Upon hearing that, I was even more annoyed than before. His answer didn't even begin to make sense. I shot back at him, "What, you wanna go play Barbies with her?!"

He quickly shot back, "No. If they have one kid, they may have another. So maybe they have a boy closer to our age to throw the ball with."

That answer did nothing to soothe my anger at him. It was well past minor irritation and up to full-scale anger at this point. I told him again to "quit staring at them and just throw the stinking ball." He begrudgingly stopped spying on that family and returned to our game.

Sometime around late 2019, it hit me like the proverbial lightning bolt out of the blue: she had to be the black-haired girl. I didn't know if my grandfather ever hurt her, but I was almost certain she was the girl in that vision. *That's perhaps why I can't see her face clearly in the vision*, I thought. I couldn't consciously recall really seeing her other than a glance from a good one hundred yards away, maybe.

She, combined with the blonde-haired girl, represented my grandfather's evil.

In normal conditions, my brother's rude behavior of shamelessly staring at someone would have embarrassed me. Maybe it would have slightly annoyed me because of the embarrassment. It shouldn't have angered me as it did, though, and it shouldn't have been such a big deal to be featured as one of my only retained memories all these years.

Looking back, I believe I feared for that girl's safety. That's why I was so angry with my brother for staring at that family. His stare could have all but invited them over to introduce themselves to, and ultimately befriend, my grandparents. That action would have put that little girl in grave danger. My fear was not conscious, but my subconscious had to have been working in overdrive that evening.

It was almost exactly one year later that my grandfather dug "his grave." The grave was located on his property as close to exactly in front of that house as possible. That family could have easily seen the grave from their front windows. My subconscious must have linked the black-haired girl to the grave. In my head, my grandfather was sick and twisted enough to find a way to abduct that girl, as he had the blonde-haired girl. He dug "his grave" right under the family's nose. He even dug it months before the murder could have been carried out, in my analysis of the evidence, telling them in advance he was going to kill their daughter. He filled the grave a good month ahead of when he said he'd fill it. In my assessment, this was perhaps due to an irresistible opportunity to abduct the girl arising a little early.

Even then, I knew what my grandfather was, even if only subconsciously. I knew he was capable of murder. I could see all these pieces even as a kid. That's perhaps why I called him out on filling the grave early.

State police reports don't show a missing girl from that area. A very helpful gentleman I spoke with at another missing child database organization many years ago warned me, however, that records from that long ago were maintained on paper, often in basements. If someone happened to pull that sheet and never returned it, or if the sprinkler system malfunctioned, or if the basement flooded, or under any number of other scenarios, the child in question would not exist in today's digital databases, even if she had been reported missing. He basically warned me that the absence of a missing child report from that time frame does not necessarily mean anything.

The thing that disturbs me most, though, is how tremendously sad thinking about the black-haired girl still makes me. It's been many years since I first saw that image of her lying dead in her white, lace dress. I like to think I have figured out where she came from and why she's so important to me, as given in this recollection. Yet I break down hard every time I think about her.

I can talk about almost any aspect of the blonde-haired girl today with only slightly tearing up. Determining that she seems to be safe today has helped me tremendously.

Through the months that followed this revelation, I tried talking myself into believing the black-haired girl's relation to that grave is coincidence. I have argued the logic of the matter to the utmost degree that those items *had to be coincidental*. Yet, I can't go back to that memory of her lying dead and shrouded by blackness to this day without breaking down.

A couple years ago, I had a series of nightmares—which I believe were completely symbolic. I didn't see people, only animals, but I knew who they were and what everything meant.

In one set of dreams, the black-haired girl was a chipmunk. There was a very large, black crow toying with the chipmunk at the base of a telephone pole. The chipmunk tried to get away, but the crow carried it to the top of the telephone pole.

I was in the scene, but only as an observer. I was concerned about the chipmunk, but she didn't look like she was getting hurt or necessarily in immediate danger. The chipmunk tried to get away again by balancing on the phone wires. The crow allowed her to get only so far, then brought her back to the pole. Then, the chipmunk tried to climb down the telephone pole.

That scared me. I began to worry, but I didn't know what to do.

The chipmunk was doing surprisingly well scaling the pole, but then I looked away for just a second, and she fell—or was pushed. At first, it appeared the fall killed her. She was strong, though. Unbelievably strong. She began limping over into the weeds.

The crow quickly descended upon her. I couldn't watch, but I could hear a fight, followed by silence.

The phone pole represented a set of stairs. The telephone wire was a hallway. The crow was one of two people. Logic would dictate it was my grandfather. He'd been well established to be this cruel. And the black-haired girl lived near his house.

There are two problems, though. Why would I have been alone with my grandfather? I don't believe in a million years I would have allowed that to happen when I was in ninth grade, the time at which my grandfather dug "his grave" and presumably would have carried this out. Problem number two with the idea that the crow was my grandfather is that's not at all what I felt in the nightmare. Following the nightmare, I believed with every fiber of my being that the crow was my father, and the house where this nightmare played out was my childhood home in Penfield.

At first, I thought that was impossible. My mother was pretty much always home. However, I recalled her father dying sometime in the winter when I was in ninth grade. It turns out, my father did have opportunity to carry out this presumed murder during this timeframe. He had the house to himself for at least a couple of weeks while my mother remained alone in New Hampshire, helping her brother and mother wrap up some things following the death of her father. My research indicates he died on February 28, 1988. His death in mid-winter may have been the impetus to fill my father's dad's "grave" early. My paternal grandfather had my father so wrapped around his finger,

I can guarantee he could make him go as far as killing for him. My grandfather would have jumped at the opportunity to involve my father in his plans, once my mother was out of the picture.

Late in March of that year, I became extremely ill. I all but refused to eat anything more than what I absolutely had to eat to maintain my life until late August that year. My mother took me to the doctor several times. They performed ultrasound scans, blood tests, and the usual poking and prodding that doctors do—and said I should have been as healthy as a horse.

Also along the health front, I don't remember when this happened exactly, but at some point in my early teens, I developed shingles. This is a disease that very rarely affects anyone younger than forty or fifty years old. It's almost unheard of for a young teen to get it and is typically associated with extreme levels of stress when it does hit someone that young. This gives a rough idea of the stress levels I was under throughout this general period.

Was this just a random dream that didn't really mean anything? What, then, could I make of all the coincidences? I added them up:

✓ My father having the house to himself to pull this off precisely before the hole was filled;

✓ My grandfather filling the hole during what was still very much winter in western New York, when he said he planned to fill it late in the spring;

✓ The grave being situated in a location where the family across the street had an unimpeded view of the open hole for months before it was filled, and forever after it was filled; my grandfather could have presumably disguised her body to look like any other bagged yard or miscellaneous waste when he "dumped" it into "his grave";

✓ The unimpeded view from the neighboring house came thanks to my grandfather spending months, if not the better part of a year, tearing out hedges largely made up of bushes with sharp, two- to three-inch long thorns–finishing that job as he had the "grave" dug;

✓ The grave site offering my grandfather an unimpeded view from the comfort of his recliner;

✓ My challenge to my grandfather about filling the hole–the only time I challenged him since he almost killed me for it when I was seven;

✓ And then there was me falling very ill for months without any physical cause following the filling of the hole.

One or two coincidences could perhaps truly still be a coincidence, but at least seven "coincidences" ALL suggesting something VERY bad happened there?

If this was more than just a dream, and my gut is correct on who the crow is, then is this why my father is almost desperately intent on re-writing history? This thought battered me.

Before I had any recollection of the past, my father feigned interest in my emotional well-being. He claimed he would gladly help me through any counseling I needed, or with any other matters pertaining to abuse at my grandfather's hands. Through the early 2000s, he openly shared stories and insights.

But when I began asking questions that clearly showed him I was starting to recover memories, he quickly turned everything around. My grandfather switched from a brutal child molester to a "civilized" father. My mother switched from being someone who rode me like a horse and would "nit and pick at everything" I did, to a saint who went out of her way her entire adult life to deal with what an awful person I was.

The transition seemed to come in about 2008 or 2009. It's a transition I've spent a lot of time puzzling over with Dr. Watson.

We spent many sessions theorizing about why he would make up such stories and try so hard to throw me off on recovering my past. *Perhaps it's guilt and paranoia associated with killing a helpless six-year-old girl that has him on the verge of complete insanity*, I ended up surmising.

What of me in the dream with the crow? How dare I not try to help her sooner? How dare I allow it to progress to her getting killed without me stepping in at any point? Fuck me for being such a gullible pussy.

Past experience led me to believe the strength of emotion associated with the dream meant it was at least strongly based on fact. The numerous "coincidences" further accentuated that point. This left me with even more emphatic questions: *who is in that grave, and was my father involved in her death?*

CHAPTER

13

The Private Investigator

BY MID-2020, I HAD ALL THESE MEMORIES and coincidences spinning in my head. *How do I now PROVE that my father or grandfather killed that black-haired girl?* I constantly thought to myself. It finally occurred to me to call the private investigator back up to look into whether or not there really was a girl of that approximate age living at that house in 1988—and to further look into whether or not she disappeared in March 1988.

I had done a little research about a year earlier and found a private investigator named Chris Holland in the Rochester area. He agreed to do some searches and reported back that there was a young girl of that age likely living at the residence in 1988, but she was still very much alive and well. He took his work a step further and searched local papers for any reports of missing or murdered children. He didn't find any such reported incidences in the area throughout the late 1980s.

It would seem my psychiatrist was right. She had tried to warn me that my vision of the black-haired girl where she lay dead in a white lace dress was too ambiguous to be a real memory. She warned me that the black background, floor, and ceiling indicated it was a symbolic "memory"—where the black background and girl's black hair likely represented death. Perhaps death of the blonde-haired girl, death of a part of me, a combination of the two, or something completely different. I was certain that the intensity of my emotions indicated otherwise, though. She said the emotions were so strong because they likely were from the real events that this image represented.

In response to that, she went on to reiterate that this symbolic vision could coalesce as much as a lifetime of hurt, fear, and anger. That amount of negative feelings would account for the strength of emotions in the "memory."

I was too stubborn, though. The emotions were so real. Her dress was so sharp and detailed. There were pieces of the vision that made me believe my brain wasn't just giving me a symbolic representation of a lot of pain and suffering. That stubbornness led me to spend a lot of time trying to determine who the black-haired girl was. I was so convinced she was real that I found mundane memories and subconsciously wove them into a horrific story. I had myself so convinced before I even consciously remembered some of the events, such as my maternal grandfather's death, that I began having nightmares implicating my father.

I considered removing most mention of the black-haired girl from this story; however, just as my brain felt it was useful to give me the vision of her lying dead to force me to confront the tidal wave of true emotions that came with it, I think the story of my trials and tribulations dealing with that "memory" are important.

First, when dealing with recovered memories, don't blindly have faith that everything your brain shows you is the absolute truth. Some memories, like this one, may be symbolic of multiple different memories—and could be your brain's attempt to process similar painful emotions from different events. Other real memories can be modified in various ways from their original forms as the brain subconsciously ruminates on them through years or decades. For something like this, though, where someone's well-being may have been impacted, I strongly recommend looking into it; but don't get lost in it.

That said, there are some underlying conditions I still consider to be the absolute truth in how I interpreted the information I gained or learned from the black-haired girl. First and foremost, my grandfather was evil enough to kill. One of my therapists suggested she's nearly certain he would have killed the blonde-haired girl had I not intervened. Since I did intervene, he almost killed me instead. He was well known through the family for his abuse. As specified, I recently learned he threw my five-year-old cousin into a set of cabinets across the kitchen for no reason other than he didn't want to walk around her. What kind of sick animal does that?! If anyone in this world was capable of killing a child, it would have been him.

Confronting the vision of the black-haired girl helped me come to terms with my grandfather's violence and the damage it left behind at every step, even in real encounters with him. I was certain for a time that he had killed the black-haired girl. That helped force me to come to terms with my long-buried emotions associated with the blonde-haired girl through all the years I was certain (subconsciously and consciously) that he had killed her. Without the vision of the black-haired girl, those emotions may still lie trapped in me. The black-haired girl also personified my grandfather's violence toward me. Reconciling within myself his homicidal nature through the murder of this fictitious girl has helped me address the pain and confusion over his beating me nearly to death when I tried to rescue the blonde-haired girl. My brain's symbolic presentation of her seems to have actually served a tangible purpose.

Beyond that, the real coincidences surrounding the black-haired girl were so overwhelming as to convince me that my nightmare was real. It's difficult now to write off so many coincidences as "odd occurrences." I'll never be able to prove this, but to me, those coincidences, my grandfather's known personality traits, and the verification that the black-haired girl existed point to one thing: my grandfather very well may have intended to kill her and bury her in that grave. He may have developed cold feet, or perhaps he was never able to work his way into the family's good graces enough to get to the girl.

I tried to contact the black-haired girl (woman now) with an email address provided by the private investigator. My psychiatrist helped me craft wording that was less intrusive and easier to relate to than in my message to the blonde-haired woman. She never replied either. Perhaps it was an old address. Perhaps people from Avon tend to avoid strangers (for good reason, if they grew up in the vicinity of my grandfather). It seems I may never know if my grandparents ever interacted with that family in any way.

The other truth the story of the black-haired girl helps highlight is the amount of pain and fear in which I grew up. The pain and fear I felt in the vision of the black-haired girl as she lay dead in the black room was almost crippling. The most likely interpretation of the vision is that the girl represented both a portion of me that died, and the blonde-haired girl's death. I say that because that vision came just before I began regaining the first few memories of the blonde-haired girl.

I don't have the words to describe that pain I experienced when looking upon the sweet little girl with black hair. My pursuit of the black-haired girl gives some idea, though, of its drive in me. I couldn't give up on her, because in my mind, a little girl had died a terrifying, horrific death—just as I thought the blonde-haired girl had. She was buried in a random hole by a man who hated her—just as I initially thought the blonde-haired girl likely had been. Her parents never knew what happened to their baby. She disappeared one day and never came home. I was the only person in the world willing to shout out where she was—to shout out what had happened—but nobody would listen. Nobody would believe. The pain wrapped in watching her die, hurting for her parents in a way only a father of two girls could, and suffering the knowledge of how unfair her "disposal" was only remotely began to touch on the lifetime of pain that came from my parents' abuse and the traumatic memories of the blonde-haired girl.

I fought hard to see to it that the black-haired girl's story ended as fairly as possible, meaning she didn't end in a non-descript unmarked grave, and her parents wouldn't die never knowing what happened to their baby. That battle forced me to confront a lot of pain and find peace at the other side of it. It forced me to process my own experience with my grandfather and the emotions I worked as hard as I could to suppress regarding the blonde-haired girl's presumed death. Once again, the symbol of the black-haired girl served a tangible purpose, but only because I would not accept that the vision was meaningless— and pursued justice for her clear to the end.

I spent years agonizing over what the girl's parents must have gone through over the decades since she disappeared. I worked diligently looking under every stone for clues as to who she was and how she died. At the end of the line, I found I was not looking on at a makeshift funeral for an unknown girl in that memory. I was looking on at my own funeral. Looking upon the death of a very important part of me that I would never get back. Looking at a part of me that was indeed murdered. Murdered by my own father and grandfather.

I'm certain part of the reason I didn't want to believe my psychiatrist was that I couldn't face the truth. I couldn't face how irreversibly I was changed by my father's and grandfather's actions. I couldn't face the fact that I was looking at a visual representation of the death of such an innocent, happy child—and the birth of such a fearful, angry, hostile, lonely, hurt one.

Findings for the "Blonde-Haired Girl"

Not only did I have the private investigator look into the black-haired girl, but I also had him investigate the blonde-haired girl. This investigation revealed she lived on Lake Road at least as far back as 1980.

It also revealed, however, that the girl that appeared to be the "blonde-haired girl" actually had black hair. In a 1982 school yearbook that the investigator found, she is pictured with long, shoulder-length, black hair. It's long on the top and parted in the middle, making it look a little wavy on top, but otherwise it's very straight. My wife, Jill, also pointed out to me that the woman in the Facebook profile picture I showed her has black roots, indicating she's not actually blonde, but more likely naturally has black hair.

I talked with my psychiatrist about this finding. Combined with advice previous psychologists have given, it basically highlights, as I stated, that you can't take recovered memories as 100 percent fact. In this case, we've found a small detail—hair color and maybe style (it may have been styled shorter in 1980)—that was changed around in my subconscious over the course of the thirty years as it sat seemingly dormant there. My psychiatrist referenced those studies where you say one thing to the first person in line, they whisper it to the next person, and it goes along through twenty or so people. At the end, the phrase doesn't sound anything like what started. She said a similar thing can happen to a person's memory as they sit and ruminate on it for years or decades.

They've all said, however, that traumatic memories are a bit unique in that they tend to maintain the original story much more accurately than a mundane memory would. That said, my psychiatrist said these memories are still subject to the introduction of error. The longer they sit there, the more the subconscious has an opportunity to change parts of them.

One thing that doesn't get altered, however, are the emotions.

Given my emotional response to the "blonde-haired girl's" attack, and the fact that I was preparing my young daughters to defend themselves from someone like my grandfather years before I had recovered any memories, it seems the foundation of the memories associated with the "blonde-haired girl" are likely real and intact. My psychiatrist agrees that the woman I found is most likely the person who my grandfather attacked. She looks like my memory of the girl in every way except her hair. Even her hair is very similar to the symbolic memory of the black-haired girl's.

It seems my brain somehow retained the true look of her hair but changed it in the actual memory for some reason. The only memory fragment in which I really see her hair was in my first recovered image of her. I had walked into my grandparents' bedroom and saw a girl sitting in that little storage-like room. Perhaps my brain changed her look slightly to help me digest the image? My psychologist told me years ago that is a common slight-of-hand trick the brain uses to help lessen the burden of a memory. In the other fragments, I'm so focused on her hand (as he pulled her from the storage room), her shoulder (as I entered the storage room), or her eyes (immediately after I confronted my grandfather) that I don't remember even noticing her hair.

CHAPTER

14

My Grandfather's Final Years

WHEN I WAS A FRESHMAN in college early in 1992, my grandfather died. The official word, as my father told us, is that he shot himself with a rifle he had owned for many years. He did not leave a suicide note and hadn't given any definitive indications for why he would do that, though. Since he shot himself, a full autopsy was performed. I recall my father puzzling through the autopsy report, looking for any clue he could find as to what happened. He confided in me that suicide didn't make any sense. The autopsy report, according to my father, showed my grandfather was healthier than most men ten years younger. It reported a slight bout of emphysema just starting to take hold, but it also said it would take years for it to worsen into something of any consequence.

There's also the matter of logistics in shooting yourself with a rifle. My grandfather wasn't a particularly tall man, so how did he reach the trigger with the muzzle pressed against his head? It seems to me that someone who planned out such an act would have left some type of trail behind if suicide had been the case.

My grandmother had been ill with diabetes for a while by that time. Her illness was progressing to where her cardiovascular system was starting to shut down. It wouldn't be far from that time that my grandmother would require more rigorous care than she could receive at home. According to my father, my grandfather had been concerned that she would no longer be available to care for the house and him. My father's speculation was that my grandfather shot himself before anyone could come tell him he was being taken away to a nursing home of some sort.

That could be how it happened. It's not hard to see that a little pussy like my grandfather, who enjoyed beating on and raping little kids, would be afraid of taking care of himself; however, there were some other things going on at the time that I think were a bit too coincidental to gloss over.

Some relatives were living with my grandparents when my grandfather died—a young married couple with two very young girls (maybe five and seven years old). Given the way my grandfather is, I can guarantee he was at least making attempts to get "alone time" with one or both of the girls. Given his decades of experience manipulating both young children and adults, I have very little doubt he was successful at achieving his end goal. Let's say one of the little girls' parents catches my grandfather in the act. I know what my first instinct would have told me to do. I know what most people reading this would have done. The rifle was readily accessible in the house. You didn't need a key to get to it; it wasn't hidden away anywhere. Even I knew right where it was at that time. As a parent, I could see waiting for the right time. Then, when he was isolated from the rest of the family, drinking a beer and having a smoke in his back room, one could have approached him with the rifle. They may have told him to go out the back door from his back room. Outside, he may have tried to put up a fight.

That's where he would have had a bullet shot through his head. Right where that little bitch was found lying dead in a pool of his blood.

One of my counselors said most police will overlook little things if there's any level of convincing evidence that child abuse was taking place, especially out in rural areas, and especially back that long ago. In other words, if someone was hurting your kid back then, you needed to do what you needed to do to defend them. She suggested they would have looked for and picked out anything they needed to in order to identify suicide as the cause of death.

Either way. He either died as a pussy, killed himself because he was too scared to take care of himself, or someone *finally* caught that little bitch in the act and made him pay for it. It's a win-win either way.

15

How Did You Succeed as You Did?

AS OF 2006, I DIDN'T REMEMBER much from my childhood before I left for college. Good times, bad times, all seemed as if they had been wiped clean. I remembered generalities. For instance, I remembered Bryan and I spent hours throwing the football around in the backyard. I remembered we played a lot of board games together; however, I didn't remember very many specific instances. Even when my brother would tell a funny story about something that happened to us or something we did, it sounded like it related to someone else's life, not mine.

Good Events

As the background chapter suggests, I have assembled a fairly complete library of memories since 2006. Along with the bad memories, I also recall many good memories. I think most of us do have positive experiences, even those who have been abused in some way. We have times apart from the abusers—or confidants we learn we can trust.

As a younger kid, I think I put a lot more reliance on my brother as an escape than I otherwise might have done. That could be why we were such good friends in comparison to some other brother pairs I knew with similar age differences who hated each other.

From the time I was very young, we had Tigger, our cat. As silly as it may sound, he offered acceptance and love that I didn't get from anyone else while growing up. When you're raised in the vacuum I found myself in, you have to find acceptance and love from somewhere. Love is a fundamental human need.

The horses that lived next door when I was very young offered another source of unconditional friendship. Although, I suppose, there was the condition that I had to be supplying the grass!

I was very creative and imaginative as a kid. I would play alone for hours with GI Joe or Star Wars figures, Legos, video games, or drawing. There was always the impregnable fortress involved that would keep you safe or unstoppable weapon that would allow you to crush your enemies. When going to bed at night I'd pretend I had Superman-like powers so nobody could hurt me. Embarrassing admission of the day, I often still think similar thoughts when going to sleep at night.

Ironically, I survived childhood largely doing what my mother complained about having to do with me: *I made the most of what I had to work with.*

Keep in mind, nothing is insignificant to a kid. That includes both good and bad things. Have you ever seen a little girl's eyes light up when she sees the cartoon dog she loves on a pair of shoes in the store? To an adult, something like that is an insignificant event; but to her, it's almost magical. I was able to grab hold of some of these magical things and make a lot more of them, simply because I was a kid. I could make a cat's love something magical.

I couldn't get love from people, so I got what I could from animals. I stuck close to my brother. He was older and typically in Mom's good graces. I escaped the troubling circumstances I found myself in as often as I could through imaginative play and fantasies. The combination of these approaches helped me survive some pretty challenging circumstances.

My Brother

My brother and I had been close for a long time. We fought as brothers do, but we looked out for each other in a way that a lot of brothers don't. I always felt close to him, and as I recovered memories since 2006, I realize more and more why that is. I'm now able to occasionally remind him of funny stories, or unfortunately, some difficult ones. The combinations of good and bad times are what make us who we are, though.

Today, my brother almost seems afraid to face memories from my grandparents' place. He gets almost defensive when I bring up the topic. He's quick to point out that he doesn't remember anything about any kind of abuse; therefore, he concludes, he must not have been involved. He'll repeat the statement two or three times, almost as if he's trying to convince himself rather than me.

He was an active reviewer of my January 2018 response to my father. My initial response had been a bit less diplomatic prior to Jill, Bryan, and a very close friend offering input and encouraging me not to take such an attack posture. Without doubt, Bryan read through the entire response, including lines that all but admitted I had been abused in some way by my grandfather. Not *once* has Bryan *ever* asked about that. What kind of brother that gives two shits about his sibling reads that and doesn't *immediately* pick up the phone to ask if there's anything he can do? In phone conversations with him, I've come directly out and told him that bad things happened out there. I haven't told him this part, but based on my nightmares, I wasn't the only one they happened to. A normal person would hear those statements and dig for more information, or at least offer to listen. He changes the subject.

My psychiatrist is fairly certain she knows what is happening in his head. She postulates that he is where I was years ago. I was feeling overwhelming guilt that I didn't do enough to help the blonde-haired girl. He may be feeling the same about me. He enjoyed spending time with my grandmother. That time took him away from me and left me alone with my grandfather. He may feel he should have been there to defend me, to take the pain in my place. She believes he may have even been aware of abuse and likely left with my grandmother to avoid it, further fueling the guilt. Naturally, he, like me at the time, was a kid doing the best he could in a horrible situation; but it's extremely difficult to see it that way when you're so overwhelmingly convinced that you let somebody down in such an extreme way. If that's the case, then in time, he may process through it as I have, and some of those memories may return to him as well.

There is a distinct possibility that he is right, though. He may never have been aware of anything happening out there. Good times may be all he truly has in his head, consciously or otherwise, and he honestly sees me as an attention-seeking liar. I'm typically such an over-the-top private, withdrawn person, I don't know how anyone who knows me could come to that conclusion. It's only because of the tremendous emotional distress I've been under for decades that I *had* to write this book to expose certain people as the monsters that they are or were— and to let people in similar circumstances know there is hope for them.

My father never questioned my brother about being abused. He never told him any of the tall tales about my cousin, or even about the real family history. As I wrote earlier, I'm certain my father was very well aware of everything my grandfather did. His lack of communication with my brother about any of this does indeed strongly suggest that my brother is right. *Nothing bad ever happened to him out there.* One of my psychologists pointed out that this is a common tactic of child abusers. They isolate and abuse the younger sibling while going to great lengths to show their "nice side" to the older sibling. That way, if the younger sibling ever reveals the truth, it's easier to paint them as a liar, given that the older one has nothing but great things to say.

My relationship with Bryan today has been strained because of this gap in our conscious understanding of our past. We spoke briefly following my father's response to my goodbye email to him in 2018. Despite being intimately familiar with my position and having an abundant awareness of what a liar my father had become, Bryan immediately took my father's response to my 2018 letter as the gospel truth. He believes my father hook, line, and sinker—that my grandfather was only mean and abusive when completely out of his mind drunk, and even then, he was "only" physically abusive. He also buys into his lies that I'm making up the memory of coming home with my face so swollen Mom took me to the doctor to be examined. He even expressed shock at my father's revelation in that same response to my 2018 letter that my grandfather was abusive! I thought my letter had made it abundantly clear that my grandfather had tormented me while we were forced to stay at their house. From where I sit, Bryan might as well have called me up, said, "You're a liar," and hung up the phone.

I haven't instigated contact with Bryan since. I spoke with my brother on the phone early in 2020 when he called me. It was our first conversation since he took my father's side. He never even asked how I was doing with the memories, if any new ones had come up, or touched on any of that material in any other way. Those events are an enormous part of me and define a huge part of my life, if not everything in it. His apparent disrespect for what I went through is insulting. By side-stepping my memories the way he is, I feel that he's implying that I'm making the whole thing up.

My psychiatrist has assured me it's only because he can't handle anything to do with that topic, because it puts far too much strain on his ability to keep his memories buried; however, it still comes down to the fact that I have to do what's right for me. My brother's inability to handle the truth is a weakness I find repugnant, and I don't need that type of toxicity in my life.

However, he *is* my brother. I have to keep reminding myself we all deal with traumas and stressors in our own way.

Suicidal Ideations

As the memories came into better focus, I found myself in many circumstances where I nearly ended it all. Beginning in eleventh grade (1989/1990), I started having suicidal thoughts. Sometimes they were frighteningly strong, sometimes they were fleeting "wouldn't it be nice if I were dead" notions. The first time it happened was one of the strongest.

I was driving home from working a shift in the fish department at a local grocery store. The road I was on was straight as an arrow and had a pretty decent hill on it. Once I reached the crest of the hill, I noticed there was a telephone pole next to the road at the bottom of the hill. It struck me how easily I could accelerate the car down the hill and swerve the front end of the driver side into that pole and end all the pain I had felt for so many years. I put the plan into motion. The speedometer only measured up to 85 MPH. By time I reached halfway down the hill, I had the needle well past 85 and buried as deep as it could go. I was measuring out in my head where I would need to start veering off the road to properly hit the pole.

Then it occurred to me. *You may only severely hurt yourself*, a thought rang in my head. *You may hurt yourself bad enough to be crippled*, the thought went on. *Guess who will take care of you for the next several decades to come?* the thought asked. *You'll be eating all your meals through a straw, and you know who will be at the other end of that straw, right? Two more years. Two more measly years, you worthless piece of shit. That's all you have to fight. Just two more years, and you'll virtually be done with her. Do this, and you're stuck with her for life. Your choice.* I slowed down, continued straight on the road, and drove home as if nothing had ever happened.

Something I never heard about suicide is what really drives people to that end. You always hear about the stockbroker who goes bust and jumps out of his twentieth story window or the kid who gets that one last F and can't continue on the way she's been going. What's really behind it, though? Was it truly a knee-jerk reaction from a single experience that led to the ultimate radical response? If it is a knee-jerk reaction to one event, is that one event more of the final straw rather than truly a single, stand-alone event?

What drove me to almost go through with it a few times in my life?

Loneliness. Rejection. Those were two of the leading forces pushing me toward that end.

The stockbroker probably pinned his entire self-worth on his monetary value. He may have been rejected by his parents, and being financially successful was his only compensation for the lack of love. When he went bust, he lost the only lifeline he had built to shield himself from the rejection. Likewise with the failing grade, the girl's parents may have based their affection around her academic success—or at least that may have been her interpretation—not around unconditional love. A string of bad luck in school may have culminated in that F driving the final stake through her heart. Driven by her parents' apparent rejection, she couldn't handle the years of loneliness anymore. She felt like too much of a failure by that point to continue fighting.

Most people don't realize just how agonizing true loneliness and rejection are. At points in my life, I was left facing what felt like the fact that my own parents had rejected me, Jill had rejected me because we were in the midst of some type of fight, and the kids would ultimately reject me at some point because they would certainly grow up and realize how worthless I was. Basically, I was certain that everyone who was supposed to love me actually hated me. I wish I had enough talent to convey the feeling that leaves behind. When you're lonely, it's often because you miss someone. They've either walled themselves off emotionally—or they're not with you at the time. Typically, you know this is likely temporary, but even so, you feel the knot in the pit of your stomach. Your heart might even feel like it's beating lower down in your chest and more slowly, and you feel worried or uncomfortable.

When experience tells you the loss of everyone you care about is permanent, those same feelings come into play, but amped up to an extreme level. Also, in addition to the other feelings, there's desperation. The longer you're lost in that feeling, the more desperate you are to find some way, any way, out of it.

A fight between Jill and me is not just a fight in my mind's eye. It's an utter and complete rejection on her part of everything I stand for and represent. I assume that harkens back to the severity of the fights I would have with my mother, and her ultimate rejection of me. To suffer through that loneliness for days, months, and years at a time becomes quite honestly unbearable.

"I'm loneliest when I'm in a crowd," as stated by the band Suicidal Tendencies, is far too true. It's easy to be lonely when nobody is around. This is usually temporary. It's deadly to be lonely when you're surrounded by people you thought would love you. Changing the perception of worthlessness you have of yourself when you were raised, being told how hated you are numerous times a day, is extraordinarily difficult.

One of my favorite songwriters, Dave Mustaine of Megadeth, put it this way in his song, "Recipe for Hate…Warhorse": "*The truth it taunts me, that nobody wants me.*" That's such a brilliant way to capture loneliness in one line. It feels like the loneliness is the truth, a fact; something etched in stone. Not just the fleeting feeling or impression that it actually is.

I've learned that it's not the truth, though. You're lost in this sea of loneliness and just can't feel the love and support of your wife and friends in the midst of that. Learning to open your eyes to their presence, to reach out and grab the rope that ties you to them, as one of my counselors put it, is critical.

It's a sea everyone finds themselves lost in on occasion. Not only are you not alone in your life, but you're not alone in that feeling, in that sea. You must remember while you're there, others are suffering the same feelings, and everyone has a rope right there they can grab to get themselves out of it.

The taunting part in that song lyric to me emphasizes the power of the loneliness. It almost has a life force of its own. This kind of loneliness is not just loneliness. It has so much power it actually beats and mocks you. It completely demoralizes you. It will own you if you don't know how to fight it.

There's another kind of suicidal experience I have lived through. An extremely frightening one. I've never heard of it from anyone else before. This happened to me once. I'm scared to death of it ever happening again. I was driving to work early one morning. I was headed to a client's site and had to leave very early, so I was one of the only vehicles on the road. I'm not even sure how to describe it. I was taken over, from my subconscious perhaps, by this nearly insurmountable urge to kill myself. It was akin to being on a diet and seeing a chocolate cake sitting on the counter in your kitchen. Consciously, you don't want to eat that cake, because you're proud of the achievement you've made so far on your diet; however, you have a very strong subconscious pull telling you that you need to take a bite of the cake. I spent the better part of an hour battling this "craving." I kept telling myself how great life was. Jill and I had been through some rough waters, but we were really beginning to get our feet under us. Our two kids were very young at the time, and I kept thinking how great it was to play Barbies with them— and to dance to *Dragon Tales'* introductory song with them before bed. I didn't want to die, yet I was fighting for my life. At the same time, I was looking for opportunities to kill myself as I drove. At the peak of the feeling, I was driving across the Howard-Frankland Causeway from Tampa to Saint Petersburg, so it would have been difficult to run into something on the side of the road to kill myself. Large concrete barriers at the sides of the causeway were likely fairly impenetrable by the mid-sized car I was driving at the time. This bought me time to get my thoughts back under my own control. I barely won, but I did. I only won because I held so tenaciously to all the things that were so important to me. I focused with everything I had on them.

If you have lost a loved one through suicide, they may have died fighting for their life. It wasn't necessarily a willful choice. Perhaps they were battling loneliness and rejection that had more of an all-consuming life of its own than most people can relate to. Their loneliness may have been a perception they had that nobody else could see.

Suicidal people, or at least I did when in that state, try to drop hints. Those hints are so subtle that I'm not sure even the most qualified person could pick up on them. We want help. We're desperate for help; but we're afraid, ashamed to ask.

If the desperation went on for years, they may have lost all strength to keep their heads above water. In that state, they thought their hints seeking help were obvious. They may have seen the lack of response to those hints as validation of their loneliness. Perhaps that strange subconscious "craving" hit them too powerfully to battle through. They may have been thinking of how much they loved and needed to be there for you, but didn't know how to go to war against such a powerful, unknown force.

If you loved them, I know that somewhere in them, they knew it—and it was one of the only things that gave them any chance of defeating the horrifying forces they were up against.

If, on the other hand, you're feeling any of those feelings in your life, I couldn't have taken control over them as I have without the help of some great therapists and medication. It's a shame that getting help for depression or anxiety has such a stigma today. For me, my brain chemistry was permanently thrown out of balance because of my childhood experiences. Some are born with imbalances. Without medication, I can't "think my way out of it" any more than a cancer patient can think their way out of that disease. It's like any other potentially fatal physical ailment.

Even if it's not physically based, and you've been through hell and back at some point in your life, a good psychologist will do wonders to help you find peace. You owe it to yourself to reach out for help and seek that peace.

In 2006, immediately following the "subconscious suicide event," I started seeing both a psychiatrist and a psychologist. There is a difference, believe it or not. A psychiatrist is a medical doctor who specializes in diagnosing and treating mental illnesses such as depression, anxiety, bipolar, and others. They typically treat those ailments with a variety of medications. A psychologist is typically known as the talk therapist. They're usually depicted in the sitcoms with the main character sprawled out on a couch, blabbering on about some goofy stuff. The reality is, without both doctors in my treatment, I never would have made such enormous gains in self-worth and internal peace.

Both doctors I saw were fantastic. The psychiatrist helped to get my depression and anxieties under control. It took a lot of trial and error—and a lot of work on both of our parts—but we got there.

Be patient. The brain is extraordinarily complex, so the drug or combination of drugs that works for your situation can take a while to nail down. Be persistent with it; it's worth it. My psychologist gently led me through getting a handle on my nightmares, pulling on threads as they appeared—until ten or eleven years later, when I had recovered a large number of both good and bad memories.

My Keys to Success

Through the years that I met with the psychologist, she would often ask, "How did you succeed as you did?" For a long time, I didn't have an answer. She pointed out that there wasn't typically a good outcome from my type of upbringing. She said I should more than likely be dead, either by suicide, drug overdose, or killed taking on a fight with the wrong person. If I managed to survive this long, she said the other most likely outcome would be for me to be an alcoholic or hardcore drug abuser. I am fortunately neither of those. That leads to the third possibility: incarcerated for something like murder and/or drug charges.

Far from those outcomes, I have been very successful in my adult life, by many accounts. I graduated magna cum laude with a BS and a double major in physics and math. I went on to simultaneously earn two master of science degrees. One degree is in nuclear engineering, and the other is in civil engineering. Both master's programs were funded by a fellowship provided by the United States Department of Energy. As part of the program, I had an opportunity to spend a summer working at the Los Alamos National Lab.

Following school, I became a successful registered professional engineer for about twenty years until I left that industry to become the full-time CFO for our family business. I have been married to Jill since September 1998. Our marriage has had its share of difficulties, but we work extremely hard together and are as close as any couple we know today. We have two beautiful teenage girls who, despite being teenagers, still enjoy spending time with us goofing around, playing games, or just hanging. They're each other's best friend, often joking around with each other, making TikToks together, and sharing stories about their friends.

My psychologist's question about how I've succeeded has reverberated in my head for years since she first introduced it. She was always very serious about finding an answer, which has motivated me to think on it. She said it would help a lot of people to know how one can grow up in that type of environment and come out so seemingly unscathed (to an outside view, anyway). She felt it could have huge implications in treating children and adolescents, but also potentially in helping adults get their feet back under them after growing up with similar degrees of trauma. She pointed out in particular that growing up with a parent as emotionally abusive as my mother is far from uncommon. You can also watch the news on any given night to get a reminder of how widespread pedophilia and child abuse still are in our society.

Be Steadfast

My mother always referred to me as stubborn. She was right about that. Even as a kid, I tended to stick to my guns. This could be part of the reason why she and I banged heads so hard, so many times. I was also never one to accept that anything *is the way it is just because you say so.* I had to try it myself to be certain someone wasn't just too ignorant to figure out a better way. Every now and then, that paid off for me, and I did indeed find a better way to do things. More often, it just left me learning things the hard way; but I learned them well that way.

This steadfastness has worked tremendously in my favor throughout my life. It leads me to put in more effort than I need to some of the time, but it helps me put in the required amount of effort all of the time. I refuse to take a back seat. I refuse to let life, or anyone, beat me. I keep plugging until I find a way to win. I've never been one to walk away from any fight until I leave absolutely everything I have on the table. Even then, I keep revisiting the fight to figure out how I can win next time.

Just as with the first suicidal notion I had, a situation where I looked two years out to where I could find the light of day, I've powered through each bout of suicidal ideation with the notion that *tomorrow's another day. Today is just today.* Tomorrow may not be everything I hope for, but I will make sure I set things in motion to turn tomorrow into something better. From there, I'll continue fighting until I realize my ultimate goal. I'm too stubborn to accept anything less.

Continuously building on yesterday helps you absorb failure. One setback doesn't need to derail the dream. One setback may add days, weeks, or years to the plan. It will often require a reconfiguration of the approach, but taking it one day at a time doesn't prevent the dream from happening. Even when the setback is seemingly disastrous and sets you into a tailspin of desperation that could include suicidal thoughts, you still have tomorrow. Tomorrow will be another step better than the desperation you feel today. It may be a step or two back from where you were a week ago, but that's OK. The end goal is still there. You will still reach it. Life will get better. Be stubborn, and keep moving one day at a time.

My stubbornness has paid off in another way. I don't take any single person's word as the final say, ever. In my home life, my mother frequently called me names like *stupid, disappointing,* or *lazy*. I sought my teachers' opinions on the matter. They told me how much they admired me through good grades, awards as simple as gold stars or as extravagant as school certificates, and of course, by simply telling me. They supported their opinion of me with graded tests, homework, and the skills only a teacher can develop in evaluating dozens or hundreds of kids through their career. My mother couldn't back up her position in any manner. I may not have seen it exactly that way as a kid, but I was vaguely aware of those arguments in some unconscious way.

Mrs. Miller, my first-grade teacher, was someone I still think of with the admiration—and really downright love that I suspect most children feel toward their mothers. She became something of a surrogate mother to me. I never felt that way toward any other teachers, but I did look up to them for the approval and respect I always longed for from my parents. All because I was too stubborn to allow my mother to be the only voice telling me what I was worth.

I was too stubborn to allow my mother's hatred to break me. As such, I found a replacement. The replacement came in the form of support from others. In this case, teachers—but for you, it could be any group of friends, colleagues, or club members that rightly lift you up and help you reach your potential. Don't settle for the feedback from a hateful, destructive person.

Be Goal-Oriented

I already wrote briefly of the approach I would take to steadfastly achieve my goals. I would maintain goals that I wanted to accomplish on a long range. Often, for the more complicated goals, I would set milestones to reach along the journey.

One of my primary, long-term goals from as far back as I can remember was to make my mother eat her words that I was *nothing but a failure*. To do that, I had to develop a plan. There were actually a few facets to that goal. The first facet was that if I had kids, I must do everything in my power to assure that they were well adjusted and actually loved me—and wanted to be around me. Second was to be ridiculously successful in my career. I needed to live in a better house and drive better cars than she or Dad could ever hope to buy. Third, I had to have a meaningful marriage.

I actually didn't want to have kids until I got married. I begrudgingly agreed to have a baby with Jill. I was scared to death of the entire idea right up until the day our oldest daughter was born. As soon as I saw her in the delivery room, I knew I had already beat my mother on the first goal. I wasn't sure at the time I could really feel love, but that day, I loved her more than words could say. There was nothing I wouldn't do for her—and there never has been anything I haven't done for her. I was in awe of her. I was in awe of my wife after witnessing the ordeal she went through to give birth–over twelve hours of labor later. The same can be said of our youngest daughter.

Having children of my own now, it baffles me even more how a parent can hate their own child as mine hated me. With the loving, supportive environment we've developed for our kids, they're now teenagers—and so far still enjoy spending time with us. While saying goodnight to my thirteen-year-old daughter just a few weeks ago, she randomly said, "Daddy, I couldn't imagine life without you!" For me, there's absolutely no better compliment in the world!

To achieve the second goal, I established several milestones. First, *get good grades through middle and high school*. Second, *get into college and ace every class*. From there, the goal became much more fluid. *Go on in school and ultimately earn a PhD*, or *go straight into the workforce,* or something entirely different. That's OK. The end goal, *making my mother eat her words*, has been the objective.

Intermediate steps can be very fluid. Going into engineering, a PhD doesn't open many doors outside of academia, so I opted for earning master's degrees. I went on to enjoy a tremendous amount of success as an engineer and simultaneously helped establish a business with Jill that is currently very successful. We're not millionaires yet, but I'd say we surpassed my parents a long time ago on the financial scale.

As far as a meaningful marriage, Jill is the entire world to me. I know she would be quick to say she thinks the same of me. At this point in my life, the only thing that can still throw me into any sort of tailspin is when she's mad at me. It's a bit ironic that I lived my entire life keeping people a minimum of arms' length away and swore I wouldn't allow anyone to get closer than that. Now I find myself completely wrapped around her emotionally, and I couldn't be happier that I am.

A very important part of attaining your goals is adaptability. You must be able to adapt to a changing playing field, even when it puts you in places of vulnerability you never thought you could handle.

Making consistent, daily strides is the key to attaining your goals. When you suffer setbacks, adjust and make tomorrow better. This not only applies to every goal you establish, but it also applies to relationships. Early in our relationship, I had a tendency of wanting to pack up and leave anytime Jill and I had a big blowup. She obviously never left me or felt the same compulsion to give up. I've learned the one-day-at-a-time approach works well for our marriage. Most days now are great, but we of course still have our fights. I've learned tomorrow will be better (usually it only takes a matter of hours, in fact). Keep your eye on the end goal, and don't get discouraged when you take a few steps in the wrong direction.

Find Good People

Throughout my life, I have been very fortunate to have at least a couple good people who I could count on to help lift me up. Through school, my teachers were always very supportive, as I've said. Without exception, they praised me when I did well and appropriately guided me when I wasn't following the right path. Every one of them deserves perhaps exclusive credit for guiding me through elementary school intact.

Following elementary school, I always had a core of two or three great friends who I could rely on to pick me up, or at least distract me from whatever was bothering me. Through high school, I had a couple of very good friends. We would often hang out playing games or go out and get drunk (which I don't recommend—in the great words of Sam "Mayday" Malone from one of the best shows ever, *Cheers*, "you only end up with two problems that way"). Either way, it was a very welcome break from the reality of my life.

By about midway through twelfth grade, I started to feel like I was losing control of alcohol. We generally went out drinking hard on the weekends, and I was finding that I was developing almost unbearable cravings by mid-week. I decided to stop drinking. I had the best friends possible, and they were very supportive of my decision to do so. Becoming an alcoholic was completely contrary to reaching my goals. Rubbing my mother's face in my future success was far more important to me than escaping reality at the bottom of a case of beer. Another score for my stubborn side.

By time I started college, Dawn was my girlfriend, best friend, and we were each other's line of support. As I wrote earlier, that relationship lasted for about five years, after which I met Jill.

JILL. I already wrote a little about my relationship with Jill while we were dating and soon after getting married. Beyond that, it's been a true blessing to become more and more part of her family over the years. I still marvel over how supportive her parents are toward us and her other siblings.

Our relationship hasn't always been joyous. Jill has the patience of a saint, though. In this case, that's not just an expression. You can't imagine how much hatred and anger I've unloaded unfairly in her direction; how distant and isolated I was for so many months, or maybe years at a time; and how resistant I was to letting her fully into my world. I couldn't even hazard a guess how many times I've projected my mother's evils done to me onto her. I've accused her so many times of doing things to hurt me as my mother would. She's taken it all in stride. She never gave up on me. I don't think anyone else on this planet would have had the strength to stand by me for more than twenty years. She's quick to point out how great I've always been to the kids and how many wonderful times there were between the relatively short-lived bad ones. She's right, but she is unique in being able to pick those out and gloss over the ugliness. She's unique in having the perseverance to break through my barriers and get into my head. She's unique in loving somebody who can be so unlovable so often. How do I adequately say how very much I love her, how much I need her, how very much I'm grateful for her?

Accept Help

Another key to my success and survival has been my willingness to let down my guard and accept help from select individuals. I've learned over the years I am strong—fearsome, in fact. But I'm not invincible. Sometimes I need help.

When dealing with memories and emotions that break your heart as resoundingly as my memories broke mine, find people you can lean on. Not just friends who will take your mind off things, but people who can truly help you set things right and heal.

I first made the step of finding help at Jill's urging. At my annual physical in 2001, I told my primary care physician that I felt very down all the time and was thinking I may have depression. He told me to stay away from reading ridiculous self-help articles in grocery store trash magazines and just move on. It took a long time for me to seek help again. It was almost too late the next time I reached out.

This is the main reason I tell you to seek help from a psychiatrist, not a primary care physician. The brain is far too complex to be dealt with by a jack-of-all-trades. There are plenty of times your primary care physician is ideal. When it comes to your mental health, that is absolutely not the case. Imbalances in brain chemistry are far from having a one-size-fits-all solution that a lot of physicians would like to throw at it.

The day I had my "subconscious suicidal" event, I called my doctor and scheduled an appointment for the following day. He put a Band-Aid on the problem, and I bided my time until I could get in to see a well-respected psychiatrist in the area. Years later, my psychiatrist confided in me that she didn't think I'd be her patient for very long. She was certain after meeting me the first time that I was too far gone, too suicidal to be pulled back from the brink. Baker Acting, which is hospitalizing someone because they are deemed to be a hazard to others or to themselves, wouldn't have held me long enough to reach the true stability she felt I needed. It likely would have only succeeded in pushing me away from seeking treatment at all—which certainly would have signed my death warrant.

I don't think my psychiatrist gives enough credit to how stubborn and resilient I have been throughout my entire life. As such, I don't completely agree with her assessment; however, the bottom line is, if I had relied on my primary care physician alone, there's a strong possibility that I never would have made it this far.

In conjunction with getting psychiatric help, I knew the depression and anxiety I felt needed more than just medication, if I were to successfully get past them. I had enough recognition of my childhood to know that a few appointments with a psychologist could do some good. Following ten years of extraordinarily consistent visits to a psychologist's office, we addressed almost everything we could cover. So much for "a few visits!"

The first psychologist I saw, Dr. Watson, was primarily a talk-based therapist. She was masterful at helping me dig into my mind to find details that otherwise could have taken additional years to find, if I could have found them at all. About two years following my last appointment with her, my subconscious started releasing another wave of significantly difficult memories—and, particularly, emotions. My psychiatrist suggested I was exhibiting some signs of Post-Traumatic Stress Disorder (PTSD). She recommended that I see a therapist she knew who specialized in Accelerated Resolution Therapy (ART).

ART draws from proven techniques from many forms of psychotherapy. These techniques were combined to maximize the effective removal of traumatic memories from a part of the brain called the amygdala and safely store them in the memory where they belong. Once out of the amygdala, the "fight or flight" response to the memories are removed.

The memories are not forgotten. The unpleasantness of the memories remains, but the life-threatening, urgent response to calling up the memory is eliminated. In other words, the memory will likely make you cringe, but it won't set you into a full-blown tailspin of pain and fear.

One of the key exercises in achieving this is reproducing eye movement similar to the rapid eye movement (REM) stage of sleep. This is when the brain typically moves difficult memories from the amygdala into the general memory. Particularly traumatic events tend to get trapped in the amygdala, however. This likely served a good purpose for hunter/gatherers who might encounter a pride of lions in a grove of trees. They would learn to never again approach a grove of trees unless they were ready for a fight. Today, though, experiencing a panic attack because you feel claustrophobic in a crowded meeting room is not very useful.

Given the difficulty I was having in dealing with my emotions and memories at the time, I would guess standard talk-therapy would have taken a good year or longer to get me to a relatively comfortable place. With ART, it took about two or three sessions. I continued seeing that therapist for talk therapy, just to touch base and make sure things remained under control, for a couple years following a few ART therapy sessions.

Long before I sought help from professionals, I was effectively receiving help from my music choices. Music has always been very important to me. The right tune and lyrics can almost take me away into a pseudo meditative state, far from all my problems and the people causing them. More important to me, though, was the message in the music I was listening to. It was the way it could tie me in to thousands of like-minded people.

As a young man and even today as an older one, it's difficult if not impossible to speak candidly with anyone about traumatic experiences. Beyond that, just try to approach someone at a party and say, "Boy, was I ever feeling suicidal last week!" Of course, you would approach it with a bit more tact than that, but the result would likely be about the same. I tried going to some groups, but the attendees were a little hygienically questionable and just weren't the professional type of crowd I was accustomed to being around.

Listening to a famous songwriter spill his guts about how lonely he is or sing a song about how he was made to be the "black sheep of the family" and take his parents' abuse all his life is enlightening. Growing up, it was only because of bands like Megadeth and Suicidal Tendencies that I knew I wasn't alone in dealing with this—which was extremely empowering and motivating. The aggressiveness of their music also helped me turn that sadness into a focused anger. Transforming sadness into anger helped me succeed and move forward with my life rather than sitting around wallowing in self-pity.

Even in songs where they basically read off a suicide note, I never felt like it was a suggestion, but rather a motivation. These guys were at the absolute bottom of the hole. They had been in the same places from which I had to fight hard to get out. Like me, they had the gas pedal on the floor with the car hurtling down the hill at over 100 MPH, ready to hit that phone pole. They bounced back. They bounced back to the tune of an insane amount of fame and fortune. I always believed that if they could bounce back from the bottom, then why couldn't I? Additionally, all of their fans must have likewise identified with the hardships the songwriter had faced. This told me I was *far* from alone in my pain. There had to be at least thousands of people who could identify with my fight connected to these songs alone, never mind countless more who would have nothing to do with heavy metal.

I draw your attention to seeking support from that kind of music primarily to emphasize that you need to find what works for you. Obviously, most people won't find heavy metal music particularly motivating. They may find this, and other depressing or aggressive music, hurtful. My stubbornness made doing the things that worked for me a no-brainer, even if "studies" said those activities should be harming me. Again, the brain is extraordinarily complex. The studies can only tell you what works or doesn't work for the people at the peak of the bell curve, not for outliers like me.

Numerous websites and even one of my therapists said I should not listen to anything depressing or overly aggressive. I cut this kind of music out for a couple weeks in acquiescence to that advice and fell into a deep depression. Listen to or read what makes you feel good and keeps you balanced, even if the experts tell you studies conducted by people who have never lived a moment in your shoes determined it's bad for you. My therapists are spectacular, as most are. They legitimately care about their clients and want them to do well. That's almost certainly why they went into this field; however, nobody will always fit perfectly into their statistics. Only you know yourself well enough to say for certain what is right for you. Try what your therapists say. They're often right. But don't be afraid to stick up for yourself if their suggestion doesn't work.

Also, don't give up on your therapists just because they get some things wrong. They need some time to learn what makes you tick, so help them.

Most important of all, I've learned over the years to trust and completely allow Jill inside my barricades. She's the primary reason why I am who I am today. She drives me to be better just by example. I never truly felt loved by anyone before I met her. I liked living in that isolated way. It was safer, or so I thought. More accurately, it was emptier. I doomed myself to the loneliness I felt because of my fears. She taught me not to be afraid. She taught me that I *can* be loved, that I *am* loved, that I *deserve* to be loved. She taught me that no matter what, she is here for me. Nothing and nobody in this world measures up to the help she has provided for me over the years. Her help completely changed me and how I see myself—but only because I was willing to go out on a limb and let her in.

Focus Your Anger

Everybody gets angry at least some of the time. When you grow up abused—whether it's physical, emotional, sexual, or a combination thereof—you will likely have issues handling the amount of anger you feel. How you approach handling that anger is absolutely critical in determining how much success you achieve in life.

When I was a preteen, I was in tremendous emotional pain. I had no idea how to deal with it. Through trial and error, I found that biting myself as hard as I could helped ease my pain. I would sometimes bite my forearm, but often would bite that soft spot between my thumb and index finger. I found my teeth fit perfectly into that soft spot, and I could really clamp down hard in there. I would get frustrated because I couldn't draw blood, so I redoubled my efforts and bit even harder.

Often, I would bite so hard it would begin to feel like one of my teeth was coming loose. I would run to the bathroom in a panic and look at my tooth in the mirror, trying to wiggle it with my finger to see how bad the damage was. It was never loose, just an illusion from the unusual forces exerted.

The physical pain replaced the emotional pain. Physical pain is easy to tolerate. To a kid, and to a certain extent an adult, emotional pain is a huge unknown as to how to deal with it. I couldn't cry. It would irritate my mother and give her additional ammunition to come at me with insults and put-downs. I stopped crying when I was about eight years old and had to relearn how to do it when I was an adult.

Jill was amazed when my first memory of the black-haired girl hit me. I was paralyzed with pain. I was sobbing unlike anything she had ever seen or would have thought was possible from me. Then about thirty seconds after the crying started, it abruptly stopped. Right in the middle of it. It was like my brain couldn't tolerate letting out emotions like that and clamped the valve shut. It certainly wasn't a conscious decision. Crying felt so good at that moment. Having the emotions once again completely trapped induced what nearly felt like a panic attack. I wanted the pain out! I just didn't know how to continue; I had no idea how to let the pain out in a "normal" manner. It took a long time for me to relearn how to cry.

As a preteen, I didn't yet know about going out for a run or doing some push-ups to blow off steam. I couldn't cry it out. I was backed into a corner with nowhere to go. Translating my emotional trauma into physical pain seemed to be my only option. It wasn't perfect. I could never hurt myself badly enough to generate the desired impact. I never was able to draw blood.

I quickly outgrew hurting myself, but even in my freshman year in college, I faced the temptation to do so. I was partnered with another student on a project. We got together one day to work, and I noticed a very painful looking mark on his forearm.

"You know how this happened?" he asked with a sly grin. "I kept the flame going on my cigarette lighter for a few minutes, then I held the lighter tight against my arm."

At this point, most normal people would be looking for the door. My thought? *What a great idea!*

By that time, I had moved past hurting myself, though. It was, however, still tempting to give it a try. I ended up shrugging off that interaction. I soon started looking back at this situation with regret that I didn't bring his revelation to a guidance counselor's attention. Within a few years of that exchange, I became aware of what his confession to me was. He was begging me for help through that revelation, and I simply blew it off. He was far out on a limb revealing his pain, and I was just another one of those people that didn't recognize the plea for what it was. Of all people to miss that.

As I got older, I began to learn how to translate sadness into anger. Looking more closely at my childhood, I think hurting myself physically was a training step in the process of converting emotional pain to anger. Physical pain naturally evokes a certain amount of adrenaline. That, in turn, creates anger. I used physical pain to bridge the gap between emotional pain and anger. Particularly for a younger boy, emotional pain is very confusing and difficult to deal with, and anger is easy to deal with. With anger, you break something, and you feel better. There's nothing as effective at relieving emotional pain for a young boy. I fairly quickly learned how to skip straight from emotional pain or sadness—to anger.

The next step? I had to learn to focus that anger. Focusing the anger and using it to my benefit was critical to my success and very survival.

When I first translated the emotional pain to anger, I didn't know how to focus the anger. I don't remember specifically how old I was, but I remember I still had baby teeth and no hair on my hands or arms, so I would say I was maybe about eight years old when I first began biting myself to translate emotional pain into anger. I was prone to "temper tantrums." I would yell and scream at anyone and anything. I would break things. In these states, I would often purposefully find my favorite toy and smash the hell out of it. That ended the anger and made me sad again.

This time, however, I was sad because of something I'd done. I could control that. I knew where it came from. I was also in control of making it not happen again. Seeking out a way to give myself the illusion of control, in an extraordinarily chaotic existence, was really behind everything I did.

To this day, triggers can still take me back to that state. Unfortunately for Jill, she happens to be the only one who can seemingly throw that switch. As the adult woman of the house, Jill, in some ways, can trigger images of my mother or my mother's attitude in my head. In particular, if she and I have a disagreement, my brain instinctively switches over to consider her my mortal enemy and superimposes my mother's aura over her. That, in turn, makes it extremely difficult for me to avoid slipping back into this uncontrolled, more primitive, unfocused rage. As far as I've come from my upbringing, I'm ashamed that I have not been able to leave those triggers behind, and I am working very hard to kill that response. These situations are especially difficult to deal with, because I experience such an instinctual snap response. There may be milliseconds to intercept the anger and do something more productive with it. I have yet to learn how to be that quick, but I will find a way.

Most of us do our best to ignore anger. We bury it. We pretend it's not there and put on our fake smiles. Where does that get us? It will find its way out, often at inopportune times; or worse, we may find ourselves hooked on illegal drugs or alcohol, fighting to keep it at bay. Instead, tame the anger. *Use* the anger. Guide the anger to success. Anger has a lot of positive potential when focused properly. For the Christians reading, even Jesus got angry, tipped over tables, and kicked all the crooked cheats out of the Temple. He used his anger in a focused, productive way to clean his house. We need to do the same with our anger.

I learned to focus the anger—like you might do when lifting weights. When you're lifting, you may picture something that makes you mad, or a guitar riff that gets you going. You then focus that energy into pushing harder into the weight—or peddling harder on the bike. If you psych yourself up only to leave yourself mad and pick a fight on your way out of the gym, you've accomplished nothing. With the anger that pain produces in you, as in the exercise scenario, don't just leave it in its raw form. This is liable to cause you to lash out at inappropriate times and/or in inappropriate ways. Instead, use it. Focus it into something productive. Use that energy and motivation to accomplish your goals. Just as you picture the aggression helping you lift more weights, picture the anger directed into doing something to make the person who angered you eat their words. This energy helps you work longer, later, and more efficiently—simultaneously drowning out the pain that you feel.

For example, somebody driving a Hyundai cuts you off in the parking lot and steals the space you were clearly going to pull into. A Hyundai is a nice car, but it's not a beamer or other luxury vehicle. Say you're taking classes part-time while you work. Instead of jumping out of your car and keying his car, you picture yourself completing that degree, getting a much better job, and driving past that sucker's Hyundai while you're driving your beamer. That turns your anger into motivation. That turns a potentially bad situation into one that's productive and growth-oriented for you.

Learn how to adapt that redirection. In the example listed, if the guy is driving a Mercedes, that approach may not work. Instead re-gear the focus to picture yourself succeeding financially, as this guy would like you to think he has; but you're going to get there with your dignity and manners intact, unlike this guy. You'll be well liked and respected by your peers and those you manage, unlike this guy who's clearly looking to get stabbed in the back by one of his many enemies someday.

When I say I was amped up by anger early in life, I don't mean just a little bit, either. A lot of pain had to be buried by the anger—or transformed into anger. By time I was a sophomore in college, I had a volcano raging within. I didn't know why at the time, but the rage was often focused on a desire to hurt men, especially when they talked derogatorily about a woman. I would hear how some guys in college would speak of women, and it pissed me off. It truly angered me how they would refer to them.

Additionally, it seems television almost daily shows accounts of someone who has hurt or neglected a defenseless child. The same was true then. The culmination of those events, along with the then-subconscious pain from my grandfather's memory, drove me to some very violent fantasies. I wanted to hurt certain random men in the most powerful way possible.

I had no idea at the time, but all my weightlifting and hours in the gym were geared toward preparing myself to defend, or even more so avenge, myself and the little blonde-haired girl. I didn't consciously remember my run-ins with my grandfather at the time, but the subconscious emotions were certainly influencing my thoughts and actions. I needed revenge for something I didn't even know had happened. I would see random guys who seemingly had nothing to do with anything. Just the sight of them would make me want to destroy them. Maybe it was something in their gait; maybe the way their nose looked; maybe their hair reminded me of him. Anyway, I felt my grandfather deserved to die a slow, painful death. By extension, these men must have deserved the same fate. They had to have done something to deserve it.

For whatever reason, I projected his vision of evil on them, and I wanted to hurt them badly because of it. I wanted them to suffer for what they had done—or what I had perceived them as doing.

No that's not entirely true; I wanted them to *die* for it. I wanted them to die a slow, painful death. I wanted to bludgeon them to death with my bare hands. I had to protect those who couldn't protect themselves. These guys needed to be made examples of what would happen if they hurt anyone.

These were fleeting thoughts. They quickly faded and disappeared after a fantasy that lasted for only seconds. They only happened a few times over a two-month period, but they show the amount of hate I was trying to redirect.

The amount of raw pain that had been converted to the highest levels of rage was staggering. I kept my thoughts focused on productive ends. I focused all that hate and rage into straight As in one of the most rigorous majors available.

Undirected rage is unproductive. You are more likely to destroy yourself from it—than to achieve anything with it. It only hurts you and the people around you—the ones who love you. You often can't avoid feeling the anger, but how you use that anger can determine what you'll achieve in life.

Too often we are told that anger is a bad thing. Unfocused anger definitely is a bad thing; however, I owe much of what I have to the power I extracted from focused, well-directed anger.

The Bottom Line

Don't take the pain too seriously. Don't give it absolute power. Acknowledge it. Let it out. But don't let it control you.

In short, I have been able to put all these experiences into writing, because I have spent years, even decades, facing the pain. You can't hide from pain forever. It *will* find you. I've actively searched for the truth both within myself and outside from relatives willing to share information.

Just three years ago, I would have been catatonic from the pain involved in assimilating this book. Today, I can fairly openly write about and discuss the past. I used to be the pain's bitch. I've now made the pain my bitch.

Make no mistake, I have broken down in tears many times writing this, but the memories no longer have the power to cripple me. Laying them out in words like these further reduces pain's grip on me.

You can do it too. Take possession of the things that hurt you. Own them. Don't let them own you! One step, one day at a time.

To get there, I practiced these approaches:

1. Be Steadfast
2. Be Goal-Oriented
3. Find Good People
4. Accept Help
5. Focus Your Anger

If I had been missing any one of these five items, I wouldn't have written a book about how I overcame tremendous adversity. There's no single facet that can be performed extraordinarily well to make up for missing other parts. If any one of these items had been missing, at best I'd be desperately hanging on, struggling to survive—or at worst, perhaps I'd be dead.

Seeking help from others may be the single most important step. A good counselor, friend, and significant other can help you find the confidence to be steadfast, one of the foundational requirements to keep pushing toward your goals. They can also help you determine what really gets your passions going. Without passion, it's difficult to lay out meaningful goals.

A good counselor or therapist can also be instrumental in helping you harness your anger and stop using it to hurt yourself or others.

Applicable to Other Areas

I've applied this approach to more than just my personal life. For instance, Jill and I have been building a business for more than ten years. Building a business certainly has its challenging moments. There are clients, vendors, and competitors who will frustrate and anger you. There are circumstances beyond anyone's control (such as COVID-19) that will tremendously challenge you, often to the point that you consider why you're putting so much effort into what you're doing.

As an entrepreneur, Jill and I have only succeeded because we've been steadfast in our approach. This has not only meant diligently holding on to what we believe, but also refusing to accept failure—and finding new ways to succeed when the old ways ceased to be profitable. Without clearly defined goals, we would have failed many years ago.

In this case, finding good people involves finding some great managers first and foremost, then filling in other positions with employees who are passionate about their field and excited to provide top service to the company's clients. Help can come from a trusted mentor, a business-minded family member, or other sources.

Finally, focus any frustration that may come your way into improving client service and working conditions. These endeavors are far more beneficial than lashing out at employees or clients—or taking your frustrations out on others at the end of the day.

The five steps to improving your personal life or business life are actually applicable to almost any smaller portions of your life, too. They can apply to your overall, long-and short-term endeavors, but can also apply to smaller areas such as individual relationships or jobs you hold.

CHAPTER

16

The "Labels"

NATURALLY, WHEN ONE sees a couple of psychiatric professionals for years, there will be at least one "label" placed on what the problem is. I've never discussed my diagnoses much with my doctors, but I'm sure they have their share of labels for me. I focus more on the path forward—and the cure—rather than the name.

I've already touched on the label that most resoundingly mirrors my past and present, but I left out important details.

I mentioned seeing a therapist who specialized in a treatment technique called ART (detailed more in chapter 15), which is primarily used to treat Post Traumatic Stress Disorder (PTSD) symptoms. My ART treatment addressed symptoms I was having as I attempted to digest particularly troubling images from my grandfather's attack—symptoms characteristic of typical PTSD from an acute, traumatic experience.

That only half describes my overall PTSD diagnosis.

Not long ago, the psychiatric community picked up on a notable difference in PTSD presentations based on exactly how the original trauma was experienced. Typical PTSD that many think of—resulting from *a relatively short trauma*, such as a car crash or assault—is accompanied by a characteristic group of symptoms. Psychiatric professionals noticed that individuals who suffered through traumatic experiences *over a longer term* had similar, but slightly different, presentations of PTSD. They referred to this as *complex PTSD*.

It didn't take long after my psychiatrist learned about complex PTSD to diagnose me with it. Some of the key characteristics of complex PTSD are shared with PTSD, but others are more extensive. My psychiatrist recognized the following characteristics in me:

✓ I suffered through flashbacks and nightmares for many years.

✓ I felt anxiety that at times could be almost crippling.

✓ I believed that the world was a dangerous place.

✓ I experienced a lack of trust in others.

✓ At times, I had difficulty sleeping.

✓ I have always held a very negative self-view.

✓ I can struggle to regulate my emotions under certain circumstances. In other words, I can become almost dangerously angry, under the right triggers.

✓ I had relationship issues that were mitigated only due to Jill's strength and fierce commitment to me. I can't even count the number of times I tried to just walk away from her.

✓ I detached myself from the trauma. This enabled me to temporarily erase entire years of childhood memories.

✓ I felt preoccupied with my abusers. That led me to ceaselessly pursue the truth about the blonde- and black-haired girls—and to unravel the true meaning behind the web of my father's lies.

I'm sure my psychiatrist saw even more characteristics than these; this list represents just the most blatant ones. I'm *very* thankful to say that I'm doing much better in each of these areas, thanks to the great work of Dr. Mary Watson and Dr. Marguerite Pinard, my psychologist and psychiatrist, respectively. I still receive routine therapy with Dr. Pinard, attempting to stride continuously toward true wellness.

If I had felt just one parent's love and support, I likely would never have developed complex PTSD. If I had just one parent's obvious love and support, my grandfather likely never would have attacked that little girl. He would have known the risks were too great—and would never have made a move. That is because if I had just one parent's love and support, I would have had *someone* to turn to after the attack. That person would have stood up for me against my grandfather, putting an end to his evil. And the agony I've carried for a lifetime would never have survived past the first week.

If only I'd had just one parent's love and support.

Dr. Pinard and I have made some recent, large strides in managing my inability to regulate my emotions. She found the likely cause of my infrequent, but resoundingly powerful and frightening, rage. Not long ago, I lashed out at Jill after she got upset with me for not liking a meal she had cooked specifically for me. It's exceedingly rare that I don't like something she's prepared. Additionally, I tried to explain to her it was due to the lack of sour cream on it, a primary component of the meal. I can't eat gluten or dairy though, so she made it somewhat plain on purpose so I could eat it. The bland taste was thus not her fault, as I tried to explain. She would hear nothing of my side and immediately fired into me for being ungrateful. Her attitude in this situation was very unusual for her. Things had been particularly crazy managing our company for a couple weeks leading up to this, and I'm certain now that she was just blowing off steam. I didn't have time to see it that way at the moment. Her response immediately set my blood boiling, and I told her in no uncertain terms what I thought of her at that moment. That altercation and the immediate rage I experienced set Dr. Pinard's gears in motion.

She said a key that was resoundingly missing from my childhood was *justice*. I never managed to find justice for the little girl. I never found justice for myself against neglectful parents. She said I'm still seeking justice. I've spent years of my adult life seeking justice for the blonde-haired girl. I've gone to great lengths looking for justice for "little Kevin" (as Dr. Watson always referred to me as a child) and my memory of him.

Despite all my efforts, though, I'm too late. I'll never find justice for either of them.

I am, however, big enough, mentally tough enough, and downright scary enough to seek and receive justice for myself in the here and now. When I feel I'm unjustly chastised for stating my opinion or unjustly subdued or put down for any other reason—as I unknowingly did during the situation with Jill and the meal—my response immediately comes as a reflex from my amygdala, or my primitive "alligator brain," as Dr. Pinard calls it.

Dr. Pinard is teaching me some great techniques that will keep the reasoning centers engaged, instead of allowing the amygdala to take complete control of such situations. These are exercises I'm happy to go through, since my biggest goal currently is to be as great a husband to Jill as she has been my wife.

CHAPTER

17

How I Define Myself Today

MY CHILDHOOD obviously plays an important part in how I define myself. The way it's defined me has changed dramatically in the past several years, though. When I would speak with a very trusted friend about my upbringing just a few years ago, it would always be in hushed tones while looking around to make sure nobody was listening. I was ashamed and embarrassed by my past. It was a past that I felt defined me as a damaged individual.

Today, I can see those experiences for what they truly are: a badge of honor. I'm extremely proud of how I adjusted to the assaults from so many people through my childhood. Even as a young child, I set defensive techniques in motion that were critical to my survival.

Through adolescence and adulthood, I have changed and adapted as new memories, new emotions, and new external stressors came and went.

I've been more hurtful to those I love in adulthood than I would have liked, but I've always done the best I could. I've taken the failures, the times I caused pain, and learned from them—strengthening those relationships as a result. I'll never allow myself to stop growing and improving on myself.

Today, I'm proud to say I define myself first and foremost as a husband and father. While we have had more than our share of difficulties in the twenty-plus years we've been married, Jill and I have taken every setback in our relationship in stride. We have come to a point where our love for each other almost seems impossible. We work side by side on our business on a daily basis. Our mutual respect and admiration make any business conflicts between us very short-lived and easily assuaged.

Our two daughters are teenagers, but as I've shared, they still enjoy spending time with Mom and Dad. That in itself suggests we (and I) have done something very right. My daughters both amaze me all the time with how creative they are, how hard they work, and how beautiful they are. They definitely got that last trait from their mother, so I can't take any credit there!

When they were little, I loved spending hours playing Barbies and other games with them. Over the years, I've consoled them through late-night illnesses, helped their boo-boos feel better, and tutored them through numerous math and science classes. As a bonus, I still get to end every day by handing out a big hug and kiss on the forehead!

To a much smaller extent, I define myself as a successful businessman today. I spent years working eighty-plus hours per week as both an engineer and helping my wife grow a business from a one-person operation to a company that provides paychecks to twenty-eight people. Today I have stepped away from the engineering world and concentrate my attention exclusively on the family business. With the newly discovered spare time, I've taken up writing books, too!

Overall, I've been quite successful in shifting the definition of myself from an embarrassment to a success; however, my old definitions still do tend to creep back in. Self-doubt and depression still sneak into my self-definition. When that happens, I try to go through my stated arguments of what is so great about my *real* definition, and why those self-doubts are nothing but lies.

Someday, maybe I won't have to go through routinely reminding myself of those things. One day, one step at a time.

CHAPTER

18

Conclusion

I WAS RAISED BY A FATHER whose apparent ulterior motive was to see to it that my brother and I were beaten—and maybe more to assure that we had a "proper" upbringing. In day-to-day living, he was often emotionally checked out. His typical response to anything, no matter how big, small, good, or bad the news, was to grunt out a "Hmm!" and move on with his solitaire game or whatever he was doing alone. As a younger man, he would "abuse" his younger siblings. He made it clear that he thought children should be periodically beaten, that they should suffer. His literature of choice at least occasionally included the depiction of pre-teen girls sexually abused by their older siblings.

My most prominent recurring nightmare was one of him slowly approaching my location. My heart literally stopped every time I heard the doorknob rattle as he grabbed it. *Was that really just the sound of the basement doorknob in a dream, or the sound of my bedroom doorknob in real life?*

Even bigger than that, he may not have killed an actual black-haired girl, but he did kill a very important part of me.

In ninth grade, at the end of wrestling season, I came home late from a meet, ate some dinner, showered, and went to bed. I awoke around 3:00 a.m. with the room spinning very quickly. I began getting queasy. Before long, I not only threw up everything that I'd eaten for dinner, but everything else came spewing out the other end. Prior to that night, I didn't even know that was possible. I was drenched in sweat, filthy from one end to another with this bodily fluid or that. My carpet was saturated with vomit, my pants destroyed in their own way. I was dizzy. I was exhausted. I was freezing cold and clammy. I started cleaning up the mess without making a sound. I didn't want to wake "them" up. I dealt with the situation from start to finish alone, because it was better than facing their wrath. I lost tens of pounds over the next several months, because I could hardly eat. I may have been traumatized by how sick I was that night or by other events unfolding around me. I predominantly remember my father as withdrawn and aloof, but memories of that nature made me question just what kind of person he *really* was. Why was I terrified of him?

My mother, on the other hand, made it clear how much she hated me by telling relatives and anyone else who would listen what a disappointment it was to have a second boy. She belittled and insulted everything I did, down to calling me lazy when I earned 100 percent on major tests, because I had only earned a 95 percent the week before. To her credit, though, she stepped up to the plate in a big way on two occasions when I really needed her help to protect me from my father and his father; she also offered a deathbed apology for emotional assaults she thrashed me with throughout childhood.

Despite my mother's attempts to help me, I found myself at my paternal grandfather's mercy during the summer of 1980. He had kidnapped a young blonde girl, about eleven years old, in broad daylight. I believe she was a friend I had made in their neighborhood who likely came over to play. He forced me to stay in the room while he beat and/or raped her.

Her calls for help got to be too much. I was just a little seven-year-old kid, and I knew I couldn't take on my grandfather. But I also couldn't just stand there and listen to her call out for help. I told him to stop. He beat me nearly to death for having the audacity to try helping a young girl in desperate need of help. The experience was surreal, to the point I question just how close I really came to dying. When I allowed myself to let go and pass out, I was convinced I was letting go to die.

One of my therapists pointed out that a man with the type of history my grandfather has, combined with the fact that he abducted this girl in broad daylight, suggests he was extremely dangerous at that moment. His history and actions that day were consistent with the mindset of someone completely out of control and willing—or maybe even eager—to go as far as murder to cover his tracks. She suggested that there was a strong possibility that the little blonde girl would have been killed had I not stepped in.

Over the past ten or fifteen years, I've faced down numerous nightmares, many of them recurring. I've digested wave after wave of horrifying, repressed memories coming back to light. The intense emotions associated with those memories brought on extraordinarily deep bouts of depression, anxiety, and suicidal tendencies. Through it all, I kept persevering to find the truth and learn more about why I have always felt the way I have. My childhood had always been a big, empty hole in my memory, and I wanted to learn what made me the person I am today.

Some of these characteristics underscore the impact of the traumas that I grew up with. Several years ago, as I mentioned, my psychiatrist diagnosed me with *complex PTSD*, a relatively new designation in psychiatry. Unlike PTSD, which is typically brought on by relatively acute, short-duration traumas such as a car crash, complex PTSD is typically caused by years of child abuse and/or neglect, among other long-term traumas.

Complex PTSD shows itself in many ways. It can cause a person to detach from the trauma, which is why I had forgotten most of my childhood for years. It creates a preoccupation with the abuser, hence this book. It makes it very difficult to sustain relationships, because of trust issues and a willingness/desire to just *give up and walk away* every time things get a little heated. As you may imagine, it makes a person quick to lose their temper. And, of course, people with complex PTSD tend to look upon themselves as *worthless pieces of garbage.*

The abuse at my parents' hands, which created this chronic ailment in me, is the same thing that empowered my grandfather to abduct and attack that little girl. He *knew* how isolated and alone I was. He *knew* I had absolutely *nobody* to turn to; my parents certainly would not help, because they were enabling and contributing to my abuse. He thought he could get away with it—all the while making me suffer along with her.

In my battles over the past ten or fifteen years, I had some great therapists helping me along the way. One of them asked how I got through such a brutal childhood to become such a success. She said my life was at least atypical of outcomes for such a background, almost to the extent that it shouldn't be possible to be where I am.

I was fortunate to receive a great education while growing up. Also, I am a very inquisitive person by nature, so even before I reached out to professional therapists, I spent a great deal of time searching myself—attempting to learn anything I could about myself and where my anger and depression came from. With additional guidance from my therapists, I have become quite good at analyzing myself and learning bits and pieces about what makes me function the way I do.

Writing has always helped me process my memories and emotions. Through the years, I have written a number of poems, and long ago, I maintained a journal off and on.

Now, of course, I have written this book. It doesn't matter the format or how good your writing is—nobody ever has to see it. Regardless of the outcome, let me encourage you to just spend some time putting your thoughts on paper. I've found it helps me by forcing me to think more deeply about the thought on my mind. This often helps me connect the thought to other memories. A perfect case in point is pulling numerous fragments together to gain a far better understanding of what was behind the black-haired girl "memory." Everything in those sections were memories I either never forgot or regained years ago. Thinking so critically helped draw them together to make sense of seemingly disparate fragments—and led me to the point that I was ready to reach out to the private investigator to finally answer the mystery about her.

Using those skills, I've been analyzing myself for years, trying to answer my therapist's question of how I thrived. I found that there were five actions or personality traits that were critical to my success in battling through times when I was suicidal or to not give in to the frustration and start binge drinking on a routine basis. Let me list them again here, to reinforce them as your takeaways.

Be Steadfast

When I set a goal or decide to go after something, I don't let anything stop me. I also remain true to myself.

You need to rely on help from friends, family, and/or professionals; however, sometimes their advice will be contrary to your experience. Don't be afraid to stick to your guns, if you know something is helping you.

Being steadfast also applies to striving toward reaching your goals. You will at times feel tired and want to stop, or you will have a setback— probably even some extended setbacks. Become stubborn enough to pick yourself up from those occasions and keep charging after your goals. Remind yourself why you set those goals in the first place. Charge yourself back into the mindset where you feel you must reach that goal.

Be Goal-Oriented

It's important to set goals that you're passionate about. Whether it's getting an education, receiving a promotion, landing a better job, reconnecting with someone, or anything else—you need to set a goal, and keep your eye on that goal. Strive to get yourself a little closer to that goal each day. Don't look at your journey as one big leap. Depending on the size and timeframe of the goal, tackling the whole thing at once can be overwhelming. Set milestones within the bigger goals, so you can reach smaller goals to keep you on pace.

It's because of the goals I set as a kid, and advancing toward them one day at a time, that I earned two master's degrees, found a great wife, and am in the middle of raising two wonderful daughters.

Find Good People

Everybody needs an occasional break from striving for their goals. You may need to forget about the pain, depression, and anger that probably led you to read this book to begin with. Finding a good friend or two, or more—or a significant other you really identify with—can be vital to hitting the reset button as needed.

At every phase of my life, I had a different set of friends—or now, my wife—but something they all had in common was that we were on the same page with each other. They were a great group of people to get together with and forget about problems for a while. I always helped look out for them, and they always had my best interests in mind.

Accept Help

If you're depressed or anxious, or just not feeling quite right, don't hesitate to see a psychologist or psychiatrist. Don't rely on your general practitioner to adequately diagnose and treat any mental health issues you're having. The brain is far too complex and out of their expertise to properly diagnose and treat. Forget about the stigma associated with those doctors. People who have never experienced true depression or anxiety will foolishly tell you to "think your way out of it," or "just take a deep breath, count to ten, and it'll be all better," or my favorite "just be happy!" Anyone truly suffering from any of these types of ailments knows those are the words of an ignorant fool. When your heart begins failing, you see a cardiologist. You don't just tell it to beat better. If your brain chemistry gets out of whack, see a psychiatrist. Period.

Focus Your Anger

Since you're still reading, then someone has probably badly hurt you at some point in your life. That makes you angry. Right? Leaving this anger freely floating around, prone to come out at odd times, will only do harm to you. You may lose a job, because it comes out at a boss, coworker, or worse, a client of the company. You may lose your spouse, because it comes out at them too frequently. The anger can't be buried. It finds its way out and often does so at all the wrong times. Use the anger. Find the anger, and establish a goal where the anger can be directed to make you a better person.

For instance, I felt extraordinarily angry when my mother would tell me what a failure I was and always would be. I directed that anger toward the goal of doing well in school. The energy of the anger helped fuel me through late nights of studying. It helped me spend hours at the library while my friends were out getting drunk. It helped me reach amazing places in school and later on at work.

I lived through a possible brush with death at the hands of my grandfather. I was repeatedly told I'd be a failure by my own mother. It appears that my own father set my brother and me up to suffer at the hands of my grandfather, a psychopathic pedophile. Despite it all, I came out a success.

I'm not supposed to be ashamed of my past. My past was the way it was supposed to be, so I could tell others. Tell them how I made it. Let them know it can be done. Share with them how I did it.

I'm supposed to make a difference.

Final Thought

Over the years, I've written several poems. Most of them are terrible, but they helped me release the emotions. It didn't matter how good or how bad they were. There's one I wrote late in 2017, though, that I felt may be a fitting end to this book. It doesn't rhyme, and it doesn't have any rhythm, but it's about as heartfelt as anything else I've ever written. It sums up this book very nicely.

Have You?

Have you experienced true hate as a child?

Have you heard your mother tell you every day—
"You're a failure,"
"You're a disappointment,"
"You'll never be any good"?

Have you wrestled with your own dad's rejection of you
and all that you are?
No interest in you as a child; no interest in your children.

Have you ever heard the scream of a young girl
Who rightly feared for her life?
Have you ever seen a grown man—
Beat and rape a defenseless child–a friend?

Have you ever stood up to defend somebody-
against a force you couldn't defeat?
Have you laid down your life—
for something you felt was right?
Have you ever taken a beating so severe—
it ended with you making your final peace?
Have you EVER been willing to sacrifice it ALL?

Have you awakened to learn she's dead?
Have you ever experienced the ultimate failure?
Have you learned what it feels like when someone else died—
and it was supposed to be you?

I have.
I have experienced them all.

I have learned to swallow pain.

> *So much it became a reflex—I even forgot how to cry.*
I have learned to cover pain with anger.
> *The only way a young boy can deal with the hurt.*

Today, I'm still learning.

I am learning to sleep again at night—
> *I'm still scared to death of the nightmares.*
I am learning to diffuse the anger and release the pain.
> *I cry practically all the time now, but only when*
no one is watching.
Most importantly, I am learning to be a better husband.
> *Jill deserves the best—*
> *She not only taught me how to love, but how*
to be loved.
> *Truly the greatest gift in the universe.*

Afterword

As Kevin's psychiatrist for over 13 years, I am delighted to share some perspectives about this book. Kevin first presented to me with troubling mood symptoms back in 2007. He was working as an engineer, was married, and had two daughters; he was well-spoken, polite, socially appropriate, and appeared superficially to be "under control." Kevin was neither fully aware of, nor did he reveal to me for many years, the emotional storms and turbulence of his childhood, which lay beneath the surface. His visits with me were brief, occurring every several months, and focused on the control of his condition through medications. He was truly the "perfect patient"—punctual, compliant with his regimen, organized, intelligent, and open to expanding his knowledge of self-care. Little did I know for all those years that he was simultaneously responding to the pain of fragmented memories of an abusive childhood, which he was trying to piece together with his psychologist, Dr. Mary Watson.

In reviewing my notes, I discovered the first reference to Kevin's traumatic memories and nightmares only in 2015. *How could I have missed this?* I thought. Easily. Very often, childhood trauma leaves its mark on victims in characteristic ways. They not only suffer from mood and anxiety disorders, such as PTSD or complex PTSD, but also from alcohol and drug abuse to cope with the pain. They tend to experience instability in their lives, and interpersonal relationships frequently follow patterns of "abuser" or the "abused." But I did not notice this kind of trajectory.

In Kevin's case, another scenario emerged—that of the "compartmentalizer." Kevin was cut off from his childhood memories for much of his life. He had literally "buried the past" and focused on academics, work, being productive—things he was good at. No one would easily have guessed the emotional turbulence stifled within. He also found a life partner, Jill, with whom he could develop a safe, healthy, and emotionally nurturing relationship. I believe that from the security he experienced with his wife, Kevin was more open to seeking help from both a psychologist and psychiatrist, and within that cocoon of safety, the compartmentalized boundaries began to dissolve, and he began to access a hitherto hidden and frightening past.

I'm Supposed To Make a Difference is a story about transformation and hope. Our past may seem fixed—stuck in old patterns of thinking—and our body parts in visceral states of pain, discomfort, or even numbness. Often, what lies hidden, unspoken, compartmentalized, and buried out of consciousness is not benign. Traumatic memories continue to damage us through shame, guilt, and confusion. Memories do not often surface as clear and coherent threads of thought with precise data points on a fixed timeline. Disjointed fragments of traumatic memory emerge in dreams, sights, sounds, and even smells—accompanied by turbulent and terrifying emotions, perhaps the most debilitating of which is *shame.*

Shame exerts its damage much like a fungus which thrives in hidden, dark crevasses. We question our experiences: *Did this really happen? Could I be wrong? Was this my fault? Why didn't I do (such and such)?* We tend to look at our past through the lenses of a child—stuck in self-recrimination and blame, and kept from exposure through shame.

This book shows us a way out. It is about one man's journey out of darkness, through shining a light on the past. Curiosity, courage, and suspending negative self-judgment are three ingredients Kevin utilized to re-examine his past.

This endeavor has been a painstaking journey, taking many years for the memories to unfold. It also was not "smooth sailing." What emerged were memories which elicited storms of depression, rage, guilt, blame, terror, and revulsion. At times, Kevin felt suicidal, but he relied on several lifelines, which grounded him throughout the turbulence: support from a stable, loving wife who stood by his side; good, working relationships with his healthcare team; and perhaps more importantly, a prevailing sense of responsibility to be a provider for his family, a productive member of society, and a better parent than either of his had been.

In writing *I'm Supposed to Make a Difference*, Kevin puts into order the fragmented memories, turbulent emotions, and self-blame which had eviscerated his self-esteem long before. He thoroughly investigates his memories, allowing room for re-interpretation and adaptation, while also challenging others for corroboration or refutation. He allows judgments to become both softer and harsher, reassigning responsibility for events through the lenses of a more mature and wiser adult. Kevin allows himself to finally feel a sense of pride in this journey of self-discovery, neutralizing the shame of his past by exposing it to light. Therein lies the healing.

While this book may end one chapter of Kevin's life, he will likely continue to reexamine, rewrite, or add on to where he has left off—to continue the process of personally evolving. I think Kevin has shown us that our pasts are not "fixed," and we cannot remain "stuck" as long as we are provided a blanket of emotional safety—and summon the courage to question, confront, and challenge the assumptions we make about ourselves and our pasts.

—Marguerite Pinard, MD

About The Author

Kevin Vought grew up in a suburb of Rochester, NY, named Penfield through the 1980's. He earned a B.S. degree from the State University of New York College at Oswego in 1995. He graduated magna cum laude with a double major in physics and math. He went on to attend the Ohio State University from 1995 through 1998. He earned two M.S. degrees, one in nuclear engineering and the other in civil engineering. Throughout school, he was rigorously taught how to write and how to give effective public presentations in order to convey his scientific findings.

Today, Kevin runs a family business with his wife, Jill Vought. Kevin and Jill married in 1998 and are more in love today than ever before in their twenty-three-year relationship. They have two daughters, the youngest is fourteen years old and the oldest is seventeen. While it's somewhat rare with everyone's hectic schedules, they still enjoy sitting down together to play Monopoly or a different board game when time permits.

Kevin is a bit of an engineering geek at heart and enjoys sitting down and watching an old episode of Star Trek: The Next Generation or any of the other Star Trek or Star Wars movies. He also gravitates toward watching the Discovery or Science channels. He does, however, enjoy more mainstream shows like Breaking Bad or Big Bang Theory. When he reads, it's usually educational material.

Throughout his life, Kevin has been learning how to deal with a childhood full of trauma. His single most disturbing memory has been the sound of an eleven-year-old girl screaming for her life—knowing that he, at the age of seven, was the only one who could even begin to help her.

Kevin is still wrestling with some of the demons. He may never completely win; however, he has reached a point of harmony with them that few can achieve from such a vicious beginning.

Early in 2020, he felt a calling. Despite his long list of incredible professional achievements, he'd always felt hollow. On January first, 2020, he learned why. Staring into the flames of his fire pit that cold night, he figured out he was supposed to share what happened to him with the world. This is why he's received such accolades for his writing and capacity to deliver meaningful presentations. Because this is how he's supposed to use those skills.

He determined: *I'm Supposed to Make a Difference.*

Notes

Notes

Made in United States
North Haven, CT
01 November 2021